GROW NOW

HOW WE CAN SAVE OUR HEALTH, COMMUNITIES, AND PLANET— ONE GARDEN AT A TIME

GROW NOW

EMILY MURPHY

TIMBER PRESS
PORTLAND, OREGON

Published in 2022 by Timber Press, Inc.
The Haseltine Building
133 S.W. Second Avenue, Suite 450
Portland, Oregon 97204-3527
timberpress.com

Printed in China
Text and cover design by Debbie Berne

ISBN 978-1-64326-047-1
Catalog records for this book are available from the
Library of Congress and the British Library.

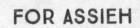
FOR ASSIEH

CONTENTS

GROW AND GATHER 149

REWILDING TO SUPPORT BIODIVERSITY 179

GROW MORE GOOD 211

INTRODUCTION
THE SIMPLE ACT OF GROWING

WHEN I WAS SEVEN, I began living with my grandmother during the summer months. She had a small homestead nestled in the oak woodlands of Sonoma County, California, on the same property where her parents built their first home after emigrating from Italy in 1906.

It was a six-hour drive for my family to get there. Eventually, we'd pass through a one-lane town of two hundred people, turn left up the hill after the post office, and continue to the end of the road. On the south-facing slope just past the cattle guard were the apple trees my great grandfather (my nonno) had planted, and across from the orchard was the old house where he once kept his vegetable garden and grapes for making wine. It was still another minute or two up the road to Gram's, yet already the scent of bay trees and the buzz of beetles singing in their branches filled the car.

After my parents said their goodbyes, the only rules were to watch out for rattlesnakes and to return before dark. No shoes required. I felt an overwhelming sense of freedom when I peeled off my sneakers. It was like a rite of passage, ushering me into weeks of wandering through woods, building forts, splashing in swimming holes, and spending time with Gram. We would paint together, work in her garden, and go on long walks in search of berries and wild mushrooms. Her knowledge of every swale and streambed and her memory for what grew in each were a wonder to me. How did she know this landscape so well, as if it were a place not separate from her but she profoundly part of it?

I often think my intense love of nature was born here and I learned to garden through osmosis, playing by Gram's side while she tended and pruned. And I wholeheartedly believe we all possess the same language of nature I learned over the summers I spent with Gram; it's just a matter of stirring it awake with time and attention.

I learned from my nonno what it means to read the landscape and work with it accordingly. He understood, as if by intuition, what to plant and where. But really, he was a master at paying attention.

Which brings me here, to this book. The childhood experiences that led to the conception of *Grow Now* and the months spent researching, writing, and photographing are a complex affair. Truly a love affair and a story of personal health, growth (with a capital G), and the indelible connection we each have to our home planet as it rotates around the sun.

There's also an elemental connection. When I was born, the doctor told my mom my immune system was weak and I'd be a sickly child. But I wasn't. Even at a young age, I attributed my good health to running around outdoors with bare feet and the many homegrown carrots I ate, pulled straight from Gram's garden, soil still clinging to them. Science reminds us of this. You'll find in the first chapter a reference to the biodiversity hypothesis. It suggests that connectivity with nature improves the immune system and protects our bodies from illnesses like allergies and asthma. It also reminds us that we need to keep nature close and engage with it, and that we're only as healthy as the environment in which we live.

Time outside is the best medicine. Sinéad, my daughter, and I visit the redwood grove near our home, which, it turns out, is quite near to where my grandmother made her home—in coastal Northern California. Sadly, our changing climate and rising temperatures may mean less fog, an essential water source for redwoods.

My grandmother's home was nestled near a ridgeline where oak woodlands, meadows, and redwood groves took root. The contour of the land and watershed allowed each of these ecologically unique areas to thrive side by side.

But that's the problem. Earth's health is failing. We can't ignore the climate crisis and the rapid rate of species extinction any longer. The decade between 2011 and 2020 was the warmest on record, and the Atlantic hurricane season of 2020 had cycled through its alphabetical naming system by the time we reached September. Likewise, the fact that we've lost half of our bumblebees and almost all of the millions of western monarchs that used to overwinter on the coast of California as recently as the 1980s is reason enough to begin repairing the damage through the simple act of growing.

You might hear people say that the state of the world's climate is too big a problem for regular people like you and me to tackle. That it's a problem for governments to regulate and only solved when the global community adopts renewable energy and sets aside half of the world's wild places for nature. It's true that we need to move toward renewable energy and protecting wild places as if our lives depend upon it, because they do. But we can also make a big difference in our gardens and cityscapes.

Now is the time to focus on the things you love and grow them, because when you grow the things you love, you get more of the same. All the good stuff, the tangible and the obvious—seedlings, flowers, food, and fun. And all the things in between that make living, living. When you do this, you also grow a more resilient planet and a more resilient you.

I've learned there's something wonderfully powerful in the simple act of growing. Here, in our gardens, we can repair ourselves and our plots of earth with our own two hands. When we then connect these spaces to other gardens, parks, and open spaces through living greenways, nature has the opportunity to repair itself and to restore its resiliency.

This book offers real, tangible solutions for improving human and planetary health. When put into practice, the information you'll find here such as how to grow regeneratively and how to plant for wildlife provides a new lens of understanding. You'll discover, just as I did, that nature is a kindred spirit. My hope is that when you notice and see—truly see—the beauty of nature, you can also learn how to restore and protect it. And like my grandmother, you'll begin to experience the landscape in which you live as a place not separate from you, but you profoundly part of it.

—*Emily*

GROW A GARDEN, CHANGE YOUR LIFE

THE QUESTIONS I HEAR MOST ABOUT GARDENS and growing revolve around where and what to plant. And it's true, deciding where you'll plant is the first order of business. We all need a home, plants included, and the home you choose for your garden helps determine what you can grow. The amount and timing of the sun, access to water, and soil quality are critical attributes of any location.

But while these are essential considerations, let's remap the conversation. Instead of first circling around your balcony, yard, or community looking for the perfect spot for a garden, let's take flight for the bird's-eye view. What do you see? Look between the buildings. As a bird, where would you land? Where would you build a nest or look for food? If you're a chickadee, you're on the hunt for both seeds and insects, lots of them. A single nest of baby chickadees eats up to nine thousand caterpillars from the time they hatch to the time they fledge. That's a lot of caterpillars! And as a chickadee parent, you need refueling too.

When you create habitat for chickadees, you create habitat for a host of other animals. These creatures, the ones you can see and the ones hiding from plain sight, are essential for a thriving, healthy garden ecosystem. It's also true that these ecosystems within ecosystems we call gardens are our most immediate touch-points with nature, and we need these places as much as chickadees do—and taking a broader, bird's-eye view informs the planting process.

If you were a chickadee, where would you make your home?

My community garden plot serves as a place to grow food and as a refuge—a hub for birds, bees, and other pollinators to forage and call home.

HOPE FROM ACTION

Since 1970, three billion birds have vanished from North America. This includes common birds like chickadees. The drivers of species extinction are complex and deeply intertwined with global issues such as the climate crisis and habitat loss; in fact, their causes are the same. Human use of the land, habitat degradation, toxic pollution, farming and forestry practices, overpopulation, overharvesting, and the exploitation of nonrenewable resources all play a role. If you think about any one of these factors too deeply, it's overwhelming!

We're not offered many solutions past voting at the polls and with our pocketbooks other than causing less harm. We're asked to drive less, waste less, and pollute less. However, Cradle to Cradle cofounder and designer William McDonough encourages a different approach. Instead of focusing on being less bad, which implies we are inherently bad, why not focus on being more good? Instead of hurting the land less, we can help the land more. We can grow more and grow it right now—starting today.

One in four birds has disappeared from North America since 1970.

Have you ever watched a pair of chickadee parents working from morning to night in search of food for their clutch of chicks? As insect populations decline, so does the diet they rely on.

Our gardens create a patchwork that has the power to rewrite the narrative while growing resilient, healthy communities and habitat for animals like our robin and chickadee friends.

ARE YOU ECO-ANXIOUS?

Are you eco-anxious? Do you find yourself turning off the radio when the news is simply too much? Repeatedly hearing stories about melting ice caps, extreme weather events, and disappearing species may bring a sense of immobility, what scientists call analysis paralysis, and chronic to acute anxiety. Where does any one person begin to address global concerns at scale? Climate change and species extinction are no small problems, so it's no wonder we feel overwhelmed by them.

While the state of the world needs addressing through all avenues, including government initiatives and international cooperation, the good news is you can take matters into your own hands. When you plant your first seed, grow some of your own food, or make improvements to an existing garden with native plants, you'll experience an immediate sense of accomplishment and renewed courage—because there's hope in action.

Joanna Letz, owner of Bluma Flower Farm, looks out over the horizon as smoke from the 2020 California wildfires encroaches on the city. Joanna's farm grows certified organic flowers on a rooftop in Berkeley, California. It's also a refuge for both people and wildlife thanks to its sheer abundance and hedgerows composed of native plants.

We each become partners, collaborators, and benefactors through the process of nurturing nature. And somewhere along the way, we begin to see that our individual garden spaces and communities reflect the greater landscape and the planet as a whole. We also find relief from eco-anxiety because here is something tangible we can do together to make a difference.

Eric Toensmeier, author of *The Carbon Farming Solution*, discovered when he transformed his 4,360-square-foot (405-square-meter) plot, about a tenth of an acre, into a perennial food garden that he could sequester enough carbon every decade to offset the annual carbon footprint of the average American adult. Now, let's go one step farther. If we follow Eric's lead and each cultivate a carbon-sequestering forest garden, our yards begin to look a lot like superheroes. Their potential as carbon storehouses is staggering, even with a significant margin of error.

Stumbling upon the community garden at Potrero Hill in San Francisco was a wonderful surprise and break from the densely packed city streets that surround it. The hodgepodge of plants and plots greets you like a breath of fresh air.

In truth, nature has shown us time and again that it can repair itself if we give it a chance. The ability of the environment to regenerate and slow, if not reverse, the effects of the climate crisis is accelerated with a little help from us. It starts with one plot at a time—mine and yours and your neighbor's, and so on. Our gardens knit together, creating a quilt of ecosystems that function as wildlife corridors and living greenways and ultimately store carbon while providing a wealth of other benefits.

Once you begin participating in the act of growing, you'll discover it's a deeply personal process, one that fosters your inherent kinship with nature. When you nurture your small piece of Earth, it nurtures you back. This book is your roadmap, guiding you with nature-based solutions for regenerating soil, fostering biodiversity, and mitigating the climate crisis. It provides you with the tools you need to rewild your home plot and cityscape, ultimately growing healthier communities and a healthier you—one garden at a time.

Together we can grow the change we want to see.

PLANET A: THE BIODIVERSITY AND CLIMATE CRISES

This is our one true planet. There is no Planet B. While we humans can't live without Earth, Earth would be far better off without us running around wreaking havoc. If you think about it, if it weren't for us, we wouldn't be facing the sixth mass extinction or a climate emergency unlike any other in the sixty-six million years since the time of the dinosaurs.

The life upon which we all depend (on this one and only Earth)—on the land, in the air, and in the sea—is declining faster than at any other time in human history. One million living beings are on the brink of disappearing forever in the coming decades. That's 25 percent of life on Earth. Food security is also threatened because many of the wild relatives of crops and domesticated animals aren't protected. We need these wild plants. They hold the key to climate, pest, and pathogen resiliency, as well as medicines yet to be discovered.

The 2019 Global Assessment Report on Biodiversity and Ecosystem Services created by the Intergovernmental Science–Policy Platform on Biodiversity and Ecosystem Services (IPBES) outlines the drivers of biodiversity loss. At the top of the list are the climate crisis, pollution, exploitation of organisms (every creature, including elephants and hedgehogs as well as mushrooms and medicinal herbs), invasion of alien species, and land and marine management practices.

Also in 2019, the UN General Assembly gave us eleven years to prevent irreversible damage to Earth's climate. Top causes of the climate crisis include burning fossil fuels, conventional farming, fast fashion, food production, food waste, deforestation, and the destruction of soils and wild systems. For example, the deforestation of the Amazon rainforest is switching the role of one of Earth's most crucial carbon-inhaling sinks to a contributor of atmospheric carbon.

The concentration of carbon dioxide in Earth's atmosphere is the highest it's been in three million years. As of 2020, the hottest twenty years on record occurred in the last twenty-two years. If temperatures continue to increase at this rate, Earth may warm by as much as 3 to 5 degrees C by 2100. The United Nations (UN) and the Intergovernmental Panel on Climate Change (IPCC) are urging the international community to contain the global temperature rise at 1.5 degrees C above

preindustrial levels. Only then can we avoid further catastrophic events such as extreme weather, life-threatening temperature fluctuations, melting of the polar ice caps, sea level rise, and further degradation of Earth's ecosystems.

In 2015, the American Academy of Pediatrics issued a policy statement warning that the climate crisis threatens "children's mental and physical health" and that "failure to take prompt, substantive action would be an act of injustice to all children." Research shows that in 2015, the lives of 3.6 million people worldwide could have been saved had fossil fuel–related air pollution been reduced to zero. The World Health Organization estimates that the climate crisis will cause an additional 250,000 deaths a year between 2030 and 2050 due to increased heat, water-borne diseases, and malnutrition. At the same time, climate-induced sea level rise could flood the homes of 340 million to 480 million people globally.

THE SPACES WE PLANT AND GROW MAKE A DIFFERENCE

There's a solution: nature.

In 2020, global climate conversations began revolving around the benefits of regreening our planet. According to the Global Deal for Nature, if we set aside half of the planet for nature, we can prevent the further, catastrophic collapse of Earth's biodiversity and climate. Of course, this requires vast tracts of land to accomplish, but it also puts our home plots and cityscapes in the spotlight. Just think of the possibilities!

We can grow habitat and connect ecosystems otherwise fragmented by our neighborhoods, towns, and greater infrastructure such as roadways and commercial centers. Every square foot counts.

During World War II, regular people like you and me were encouraged to help carry the burden of the war by growing their own fruits, vegetables, and herbs.

LEFT: Even a patch of sunflowers and milkweed makes a difference, providing forage and habitat—plus you get flowers! **RIGHT:** Milkweed is a critical host plant for western monarchs. As of fall 2020, there were fewer than two thousand western monarch individuals overwintering in California where they once numbered in the millions.

GROW NOW.
WHAT YOU PLANT FOR TOMORROW
YOU GROW TODAY.

PRINCIPLES FOR NATURE-BASED SOLUTIONS

When we consider nature-based solutions through the lens of restoring habitat to our growing spaces, it's important to keep the following, guiding principles in mind:

- Get to know the layers of systems within the greater ecosystem of your home, community, and region.

- Consider what ecosystem services your homescape, plot, or landscape provides. Think about its strengths, and where it needs uplifting and regenerating.

- Find simple ways to connect the space you're tending to other nearby areas to create living greenways. Plant a tree for birds such as an oak, a hawthorn, or a dogwood, and consider growing flowering plants like milkweed and sage in your kitchen garden.

- Develop short- and long-term actionable goals that include a vision for maintenance with the understanding that living systems evolve and change, and you will evolve and change in the process.

BENEFITS OF NATURE-BASED SOLUTIONS

biodiversity

food security

clean air

clean water

resource and carbon cycling

water filtration and storage

flood and erosion control

climate regulation

individual well-being

healthy families

resilient communities

Gardening became a community effort across the globe. Front lawns, window boxes, parks, vacant lots, baseball fields, and even zoos were transformed into food hubs.

Australia and the United Kingdom launched Dig for Victory campaigns, and allotments (places where community members come together to tend individual plots of land) in the UK nearly doubled to 1,400,000. At the same time, residents of Canada and the United States planted victory gardens of their own. By 1943, people in the US had planted more than twenty million gardens in which roughly two-thirds

ROLES AND BENEFITS OF NATURE-BASED SOLUTIONS

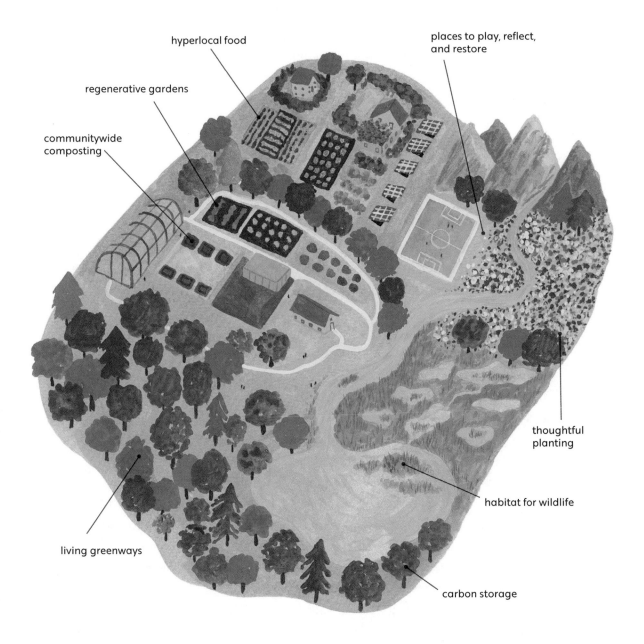

hyperlocal food

places to play, reflect, and restore

regenerative gardens

communitywide composting

thoughtful planting

habitat for wildlife

living greenways

carbon storage

Growing a healthy planet happens one plot at a time with the help of nature-based solutions to grow habitat and connect ecosystems.

of households grew 10 million tons of food. This equates to approximately 40 percent of all the fresh food consumed in the States at the time. Needless to say, the movement was a huge success. Yet, following the war, many of the gardens were abandoned with the advent of conventional farming and a booming food supply. Now is the time to bring them back, but this time with a renewed perspective and set of tools that help us go beyond organic.

According to the United Nations, nature-based solutions such as **rewilding** have the potential to provide more than a third of the remedies needed to stabilize our warming planet in the next ten years.

CHANGE STARTS AT HOME

The opportunity to grow change is right here under our feet. Victory gardens successfully brought communities together while aiding the war effort. Now we have a similar opportunity, but with the goal of growing health, happiness, and a resilient planet.

Did you know that according to the National Wildlife Federation, 1 million acres of habitat are lost to suburban development every year? Single-family homes are getting bigger, and the lawns and nonnative plants so commonly added to newly modified landscapes don't support wildlife and do little to sustain essential soil ecosystems and clean waterways. It's safe to say that somewhere in our effort for progress, a disconnect has developed. Instead of bringing nature home, we have inadvertently shut nature out.

To make sense of this, I find it helpful to remember a saying attributed to Henry Ford: "If you always do what you've always done, you'll always get what you've always got." In some cases this isn't a bad thing. Like your morning walk— Isn't it one of the best ways to start the day? But in other cases, the status quo is a set of self-defeating habits that never end well—very much like our historic approach to landscapes.

Yet, it's incredible what a simple shift in perspective can offer. Dr. Claudia Gross, founder of the speakGreen blog and author of *Words Create Worlds*, asks us to consider language as a tool for changing the world. She's certain that through

It's often the case that your garden is your closest opportunity to connect with nature and rewild your community.

The community garden at Potrero Hill in San Francisco is an oasis of green, ultimately providing an important island of habitat for wildlife and people.

"the language we speak, we are co-creating our futures . . . so the moment we are transforming our language, we can transform the world."

This is why words like *rewild*, *restore*, *revive*, *resilient*, and *regenerate* are so important. Words like these allow you to rewire your approach to the land-scape—and yourself—through language while acquiring the tools for making these words reality.

NURTURE YOUR NATURE

As kids, most of us played in the dirt. I'm sure you did too. Why did you ever stop?

Your childhood infatuation with dirt is akin to nutritional wisdom. You instinctively knew that soil is good for you—its smell intoxicating. It wasn't a love affair that needed words or explanations but one that was expressed through action. Why else would the nearly uncontrollable desire to push your hands through the earth take over?

Research suggests that soil microbes are essential for your personal well-being and the well-being of the planet. They boost your immune system and make you feel happy and less anxious and stressed.

Simply spending twenty minutes a day in nature improves the health of both your mind and body. If you don't have open space nearby, you can grow it in the spaces closest to home.

What's interesting is, the ingredients in soil that inspire this need are the same ingredients that have the power to mitigate the climate crisis, ease species extinction, and help heal the planet: microbes. When we protect and feed soil microbes with the simple act of growing using the principles in this book, we enable them to thrive. We then ride on their coattails, because the more resilient the soil ecosystem and the microbes that inhabit it, the more resilient you and I are too.

The collection of bacteria, fungi, viruses, and protozoa (together considered microbes) that live in and on the human body is your **microbiome**. What's fascinating is that the human microbiome contains two hundred times more microbial genes than human genes—we are more microbe than human!

You know that feeling when you step into a garden, park, or nearby nature preserve? The air is fresh, you're surrounded by leafy things, and a sense of peace and clarity washes over you. This feeling is an expression of your nature connection. Being in nature is like rebooting with the mothership because, quite literally, you are nature—*we are nature*. Scientific study after study connects the dots between time spent outside and a healthy body and mind. Conversely, studies point to increased depression and anxiety rates when there's a break in this connection, as if being separated from an old friend.

Simply spending 120 minutes a week in nature improves the health of both your mind and body, like getting your recommended daily allowance of vegetables. Nature provides "vitamins" and reduces your risk of cardiovascular disease, type 2 diabetes, high blood pressure, depression, anxiety, and stress. It also improves immune function, elevates mood, and increases your overall sense of well-being— meaning you're healthier and happier, and all the good mood systems are firing thanks to time outside.

But there's something deeper here—we've coevolved with nature. The genetic imprint of nature within each of us is as much a language of the mind as it is of the body. While the physical benefits of being outside can be attributed simply to moving our bodies, the layers of this onion are, quite literally, alive and teaming with microbes—very much like soil.

In fact, just like soil is filled with microbes, you are too. All that stuff about the soil ecosystem and the planetary system—well, your body is a reflection of these same systems, just scaled down into a neat package that is part human, part microbe.

THE BIODIVERSITY HYPOTHESIS

Microbes are our coconspirators, teaching our bodies the language of the natural world: how to recognize, decode, and distill nature on a genetic level so what we encounter in the environment is interpreted as an old friend, not something to mount a defense against (think allergic reaction). Scientists use the "old friends" hypothesis or, more recently, the biodiversity hypothesis to explain the connection.

The biodiversity hypothesis proposed by Tari Haahtela of the University of Helsinki in Finland is both a win for understanding how to improve personal health and a cautionary tale. It encourages each of us to "take nature close, to touch, eat, breathe, experience and enjoy" it to improve well-being, going on to argue that contact with nature enlivens the human microbiome. The more biodiverse the environment (sometimes referred to as the greater biome), the more biodiverse is your personal microbiome (or gut) and, therefore, the more robust and resilient your immune system and its ability to protect the body from inflammatory disorders such as allergies and asthma. Sadly, the quickened pace of biodiversity loss on our home planet due to the climate crisis, urbanization, and fragmentation of habitats is deteriorating this age-old path to wellness.

The background of this hypothesis is instructive. During World War II, the Finnish province of Karelia was fought over and divided, with a large portion of it ceded to the Soviet Union. Keep in mind that this area was a single cultural region. However, following the war, people living on the Russian side of the border continued to live a traditional, rustic life much as they had before the political tensions and division, while the Finnish side modernized. From this new cultural divide grew a set of data that drew the attention of researchers.

Spending time outside populates your body with nature's microbes and improves your immune function.

Why is it that people on the Finnish side now have a significantly higher rate of autoimmune and inflammatory disorders than those on the Russian side? Conditions such as asthma, allergies, and other inflammatory diseases are ten times higher on the Finnish side.

The reason is: microbes. Specifically, exposure to environmental microbes beginning early in life is critical for healthy immune function, with exposure to a group of microbes commonly found in soil called *Acinetobacter* playing a central role. Additional studies conducted by leading immunologists at the University of Helsinki found that microbes from plants are equally as valuable in the development of our immune responses.

When we spend time outside in highly biodiverse environments (think greenbelts, forests, meadows, organic farms, and gardens), our bodies populate with

TOP: My friend Nicky in her garden. The food she grows and the space itself are touchpoints with nature. **ABOVE:** How do you feel about spiders? Whether you love them or not, they're essential to a thriving garden and ecosystem. They're fascinating too. This crab spider can change color to match the flower it's visiting.

nature's microbes, and it's these microbes that provide us with protection while helping our bodies interpret the world around us.

What does this have to do with growing things, protecting biodiversity, and sequestering carbon in soil? Everything. Soil health and successful carbon storage is a direct function of its biodiversity, just as human health is a direct function of biodiversity.

YOUR NATURE QUOTIENT

Look up, look down, look all around. What do you see? What are the fragrances and sounds you smell and hear? Is there a home for chickadees—and a biodiverse range of other creatures—in the spaces past your windows and down your lane and city streets? Is there habitat for people as well as wildlife? To understand what this habitat looks like and how to cultivate it, start by assessing your nature quotient.

Your nature quotient (NQ) is a measure of your understanding of the natural world, the dynamics at work within it, and your personal connectivity to nature. In contrast, your intelligence quotient (IQ) is a measure of your ability to reason, and your emotional quotient (EQ) is a measure of your ability to understand and work cooperatively with others. EQ involves skills such as self-awareness, motivation, and empathy. Some say your EQ is a far better measure of your ability to succeed in life than your IQ, but very few reference the importance of your NQ.

The development of a high NQ comes from spending time in nature. It involves skills such as observation, curiosity, mindfulness, and, like with EQ, empathy and compassion. It's not a measure of the number of animals and plants you can identify by name so much as of your ability to discern the uniqueness and interconnectedness of nature through the power of observation. Ultimately, a high NQ renders a deep understanding of your connectivity with the natural world and a sense that you don't exist outside of it but flourish within it. A high NQ's side effects include lower blood pressure, less stress, and improved all-around well-being.

Take the "Measure Your NQ" quiz to help frame your thinking as you move through the pages of this book. If you were to grade yourself, how would you score? Do you consider yourself a person with a high NQ, or is this an area you'd like to devote some time to? It's helpful to understand too that your NQ is your benchmark for nurturing your nature, which ultimately holds the key to solving the climate crisis and species extinction—and a thriving garden.

MEASURE YOUR NQ

Circle all that apply.

- **How much time, on average, do you spend outside each week?**
  two+ hours | one hour | less than one hour

- **What are your touchpoints with nature?**
  houseplants | nearby park or open space | plants and trees in your yard | garden

- **Which of the following have you done recently?**
  take a nature walk | stop when you hear the sound of a bird | notice a change in wind direction | look to the sun to figure out the time of day | notice a shift in seasons | pick up litter | photograph flowers and plants

- **How often do you feel burnt out and exhausted?** *often | sometimes | never*

- **How comfortable are you without Wi-Fi? Or going without your phone for periods of time?**
  love it | hate it | doesn't matter | a mix of all three

- **Can you determine when the moon is full?** *yes | no*

- **What do you think of bugs?** *frightening | fascinating*

- **What are your feelings on dirt?** *love it | hate it | neutral | not sure*

- **What do you do when you find spiderwebs outside?**
  leave them where you find them | swipe them away

- **How do you see yourself?**
  as someone who can grow anything with a little bit of effort | as someone with a black thumb and everything you try to grow withers

Robert Hewitt, of the landscape design firm Girasole Sonoma, transformed his front yard into a sanctuary for people and wildlife. If you were a bird, butterfly, or bee, where would you live?

15 EASY WAYS
TO INCREASE YOUR NQ

1 Keep a bird book and binoculars by the window.

2 Grow three new herbs in your kitchen or on your patio.

3 Compost your kitchen scraps and yard waste.

4 Try growing—from a cutting—a plant you pass on walks in your neighborhood.

5 Try propagating a favorite houseplant.

6 Try growing mushrooms in your cupboard or in a shady spot outside. Maybe even in a nearby park.

7 Commit to using only organic fertilizers.

8 Follow the sun by creating outdoor spaces to be in either sun or shade, depending on the season.

9 Add a new, pollinator-friendly planting bed to your existing garden.

10 Begin a nature project. What can you make with leaves, driftwood, or other found items?

11 Do a simple test of the soil near your home.

12 Plan a small cutting garden for homegrown bouquets.

13 If there are trees in your yard or nearby landscape, create a comfortable spot to sit and enjoy them for some at-home forest bathing.

14 Replace a section of your lawn with a riot of regionally appropriate plants and wildflowers.

15 Fill window boxes and planters with flowers and leafy greens you've never planted before.

BRING NATURE HOME: GROW A GARDEN

Feed the soil Add organic mulch and compost to the soil surface, plant perennials, and maintain living roots in the ground to feed the soil, sequester carbon, reduce flood risk, and provide habitat for insects, birds, and other animals throughout the seasons.

Scrap your lawn and embrace a garden jungle Lawns are water hogs and often rely on chemical inputs such as synthetic fertilizers that harm insects and microbes, and ultimately leach into groundwater and waterways.

Grow native plants Did you know that many bees are specialists and visit the native plants with which they've coevolved?

Foster biodiversity with diversity Landscapes and gardens planted with a diverse range of native perennials, edibles, and select ornamentals foster biodiversity and provide a plethora of ecosystem services from which we all benefit. A diversity of plantings creates a resilient, robust system that requires fewer inputs.

Create homes for wildlife Make room for toads, native bees, birds, butterflies, and the many other creatures with whom you share your community.

THE POWER OF OUR PATCHWORK OF GARDENS

According to the US Forest Service, 6,000 acres of open space is developed in the United States each day. If development continues at its current rate, it's projected that the total developed land area in the United States will increase by 39 to 69 million acres between 2010 and 2060.

How can we provide the conditions necessary to enable nature to repair damaged and fragmented ecosystems? We can think of our gardens as nature-based, biodiversity-building hubs for rewilding healthy communities and growing positive change.

Let's do the math. Add parcel upon parcel dedicated to suburban lots, lawns, hellstrips, rooftops, and forgotten corners, and now we're working with something sizeable. The United States has nearly 139 million acres of privately held land dedicated to residential living. This is an area roughly four times as large as the state of New York. Now turn your attention to similar parcels in the UK, Europe, Australia, Japan, and on until we stretch across the globe. Collectively we can rewild the spaces closest to home and create habitat while decreasing our carbon footprint and increasing stable carbon stores with regenerative, no-dig practices.

In practice, rewilding is a form of back-to-nature conservation promoting natural systems while creating bridges and living greenways to reconnect habitat. When we approach a landscape with rewilding in mind, we're giving nature room to do what nature does best: grow! In the process, we're growing more good while rewilding ourselves.

It begins with paying attention and nurturing your NQ. It then continues with thoughtful planning, planting, and commonsense soil care practices.

GO BEYOND ORGANIC

NATURE-BASED SOLUTIONS BEGIN WITH CARBON. Yet, *carbon* has become a dirty word thanks to its ever-growing abundance in Earth's atmosphere, where it's headed toward devastating levels. What we forget is that it's an essential building block of life, and one of its primary homes is in the ground. How do we put excess atmospheric carbon back into the ground? By growing plants and caring for the soil in which they grow.

While this may sound far too simple, it's true. It's simple solutions that often offer the best, most promising answers. When I was in college, my botany professor, Dr. Michael Mesler, espoused the merits of simplicity with the concept of parsimony (also known as Occam's razor). When explaining relationships in evolutionary biology, he would say, "Parsimony shows us that life is connected in the simplest, most economical ways." The least complicated explanation of how species are related is usually the best, most likely explanation. He even went so far as to describe parsimony as elegant.

For me, this illuminated a dark corner of understanding. Since then, my approach to life has transformed thanks to the concept of parsimony. Why overcomplicate things—anything—when it's unnecessary and potentially counterproductive?

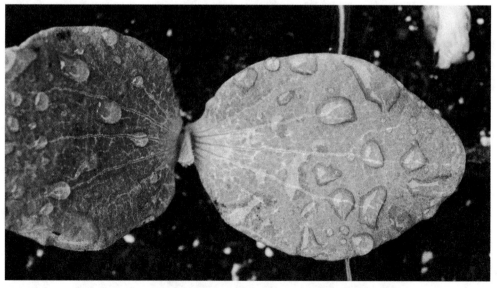

Seeds are naturally "elegant." Most of what a seed needs to get its start is found within the seed itself: the starches and proteins in the seed's endosperm, what I often refer to as its lunch box, and the plant itself. Give them moisture, warmth, and a place to grow, and seedlings like this pumpkin sprout thrive.

If we apply parsimony to the climate crisis, nature-based solutions become self-evident. Consider this. We can build and employ energy-consuming carbon-scrubbing machines to remove atmospheric CO_2 or we can plant seeds, care for the soil, and foster biodiversity, which, in turn, naturally captures and stores carbon from the atmosphere. Which sounds more elegant to you?

CARBON CYCLING BASICS

With gardening, we're urged first to consider nitrogen, phosphorus, and potassium (N-P-K) ratios to feed and care for plants because they're essential macronutrients for proper plant growth. You can find N-P-K ratios on bags of fertilizer, soil mix, and compost. Carbon is also a key macronutrient needed to feed soil, but it generally goes unlisted except as ingredients such as tree fibers, rice hulls, and bark.

Carbon is the main ingredient in soil organic matter and gives soil its structure, fertility, and water-holding capacity. We take its presence for granted, yet it's carbon that drives the life cycle, providing the foundation for life as we know it.

It all starts with the sun.

When scientists look for signs of life out among the stars, they first look for potentially habitable planets with the presence of water and then search for signs of **carbon-based life**. There are more than ten million carbon-based compounds in living things, falling into four main groups: carbohydrates, fats and oils, proteins, and DNA. Indeed, the building blocks of life as we know it. Carbon is life.

Energy is transformed via photosynthesis
Plants trap solar energy and breathe in carbon dioxide (CO_2) from the atmosphere. Water (H_2O) and CO_2 then react chemically (thanks to the presence of solar energy). Glucose (a simple sugar and form of carbohydrate) is formed, and oxygen (O_2), a by-product of photosynthesis, is exhaled back out to the atmosphere. Light energy + carbon dioxide + water = glucose + oxygen. Glucose (sugar) is carbon.

Garden soil is teeming with microbes that shuttle nutrients and moisture to plants.

Plants and soil microbes (bacteria and fungi) share resources Some of the carbon (glucose) created during photosynthesis is used right away for plant growth and metabolism. Other carbon is funneled along with a host of other plant-made compounds into and out of roots. They're considered "root exudates"—a fancy term to describe the currency plants use to barter for precious resources, such as nutrients and water, mined by soil microbes. Roots exude carbohydrates and organic acids into soil.

Soil stores carbon Like with plants, some of the carbon entering the soil is consumed immediately by soil life. This carbon, found initially in the upper levels of the ground near the surface, is fuel for microbes such as bacteria and fungi. While much of this carbon is respired back out to the atmosphere (think decomposition), some lingers in the soil as stable soil

CARBON CYCLE IN REVIEW

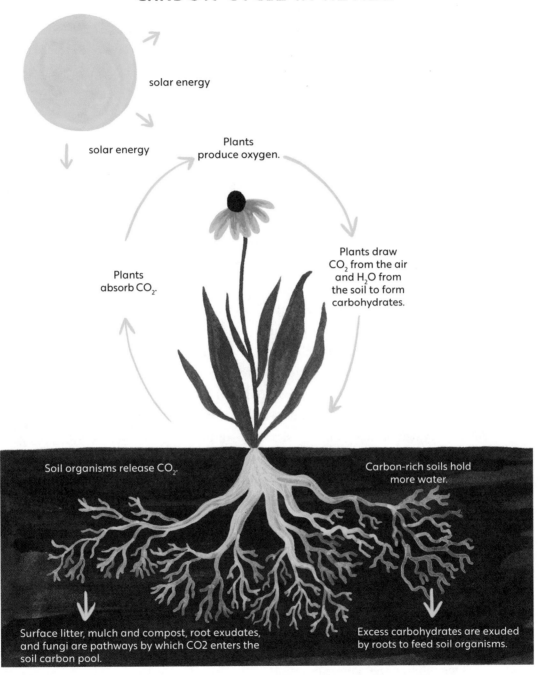

solar energy

solar energy

Plants
produce oxygen.

Plants draw
CO_2 from the air
and H_2O from
the soil to form
carbohydrates.

Plants
absorb CO_2.

Soil organisms release CO_2.

Carbon-rich soils hold
more water.

Surface litter, mulch and compost, root exudates,
and fungi are pathways by which CO2 enters the
soil carbon pool.

Excess carbohydrates are exuded
by roots to feed soil organisms.

Magic in the dirt. Leaf litter, compost, organic mulches, root exudates, and fungi are pathways for CO_2 to enter
the soil carbon pool.

carbon, protected and hidden in small aggregates of soil particles where it can persist for a hundred years or more. This is humus—that stuff that's wonderfully rich and deep brown and smells of earthy goodness.

Feeding carbon to soil sequesters CO_2 and fosters life. When we feed the soil with compost and other organic, carbon-rich amendments, we're in truth feeding soil microbes. Microbes then shuttle precious nutrients and moisture to plants, acting as a superhighway of communication and nutrient exchange between plants while driving the carbon cycle through the soil ecosystem. Collectively these processes foster life both above and below the ground.

REVIVE. RESTORE. REGENERATE.

When beginning to rewire your approach to gardening, it's helpful to remember that soil is a carbon sink. The top meter (about a yard) of the world's soils holds three times more carbon than the atmosphere! Yet, since the advent of agriculture some twelve thousand years ago, Earth's soils have lost roughly 133 billion metric tons of carbon from the top 2 meters, with nearly half of these tons lost since the start of the Industrial Revolution.

In real-world, everyday terms, think of soil carbon as the organic matter held by soil. Leaves, twigs, dead animals, poop, compost, bits of wood, bark, and other remnants of life are organic matter provided for free by nature. Soil carbon exists well below the top layers of soil (what scientists refer to as the O and A soil horizons), and our goal is to consider moving carbon into and below these initial layers.

A single teaspoon of rich **garden soil contains more microbes** than there are people on Earth. In fact, according to nematologist Kathy Merrifield of Oregon State University, this one teaspoon "can hold up to one billion bacteria, several yards of fungal filaments, several thousand protozoa, and scores of nematodes."

While the loss of soil carbon to the atmosphere is significant, it's not reason to give up—quite the opposite. Nature has shown us time and again it can repair itself when given the opportunity.

I came across this abandoned farmhouse in Wisconsin with telltale signs of its previous owners: a set of golf clubs, glass jars filled with nails, a watering can. While not that long ago a family lived here, the barn and surrounding property is now home to a budding forest.

Some thirty years following the 1986 nuclear power plant disaster in Chernobyl, researchers discovered that the surrounding area had become an "accidental nature reserve." Here, woodlands have swallowed up buildings, and all but the most vulnerable plant and animal species have returned with abandon. What's astounding, more wildlife has been found there after the disaster than in the years prior.

Similarly, during the coronavirus pandemic, measures designed to limit our own species' movement gave wild species room to stretch and breathe. Leatherback turtles began repopulating beaches in Thailand. Coyotes expanded their range across the Golden

How much carbon can we return to soil and at what rate? There's still much work to be done to understand the actual carbon-storing capacity of soil. Researchers have found that **soil carbon storage varies** by region, climate, and soil type and is a process that often takes decades, reminding us of the urgency to Grow Now to grow a better future.

Gate Bridge, and roadside verges in the UK left uncut gave rare wildflowers and bees a chance to repopulate in places otherwise perfectly mown.

Soil can rebound, too, if we give it room to breathe and carbon to eat. When we reframe the how-to's of growing and feeding a garden to growing and feeding soil, a whole bunch of problems are solved.

REGENERATIVE ORGANIC AGRICULTURE FOR HOME GARDENS

There's a growing trend in agriculture we can support and adopt in our home gardens and communities that returns carbon back to soil, reduces carbon emissions, and helps restore the soil ecosystem while fostering biodiversity. It's commonly referred to as regenerative organics or carbon gardening, but really these are new terms for an age-old set of techniques. We've simply brought them back into fashion, sort of like bell-bottoms and crop tops of the '70s, but way cooler.

When we care for soil, we're caring for the greater ecosystem—not only plants but biodiversity as a whole.

Chris Noyd, an employee of Community Market Natural Foods in Santa Rosa, California, is collaborating with the Steele & Hops Public House across the street to revive the abandoned planting area adjacent to the Public House building. The area looked barren when she began, and she's slowly regenerating one section at a time beginning with a healthy 6-plus-inch (15-centimeter) layer of compost.

In the simplest terms, regenerative organics (RO) is a holistic, nature-based approach to farming with the primary focus of caring for soil and soil ecosystems. Improving soil health through RO principles increases the carbon-storing capacity of soil while increasing biodiversity. If you remember the underpinnings of the biodiversity hypothesis, the healthier and more biodiverse the environment, including the soil environment, the healthier and more resilient your personal environment and the environment as a whole.

Other aspects of regenerative organic agriculture include concerns such as animal welfare and worker fairness. At the homescape level, this translates into caring for the wildlife inherent in our systems, making room for rare wildlife to return, encouraging pollinators, and even caring for mini farm animals like chickens.

Social justice issues are also addressed. When we return the power of food growing back to people and neighborhoods, we inherently improve localized food access while growing more resilient communities. Nature is returned to communities, too, healing the bonds broken through environmental injustices.

HOW REGENERATIVE GARDENING WORKS

Together, plant roots and soil microbes form a complex underground superhighway. This is the pathway for sharing water and nutrients and moving carbon along the carbon cycle journey, where some of it is left behind in the form of stable soil aggregates or what we call humus.

Plants with **mycorrhizal relationships** transfer up to 15 percent more carbon to soil than non-mycorrhizal plants.

Approximately 90 percent of all plants form symbiotic relationships with soil-dwelling fungi that ultimately increase the surface absorbing area of the roots. These mycorrhizal fungi produce a sticky substance called glomalin that's essential for building soil structure and storing carbon, creating stable soil carbon protected within soil aggregates. The filaments or hyphae of mycorrhizal fungi, also coated in glomalin, extend plants' reach, increasing access to vital nutrients and water.

A regenerative, no-dig, or no-till approach protects this soil system and soil structure while keeping soil carbon stable and underground. While there's still

Regenerative gardening incorporates a no-dig approach and a diverse range of plantings.

some digging in a no-dig garden, it's strategic. Soil is covered with organic matter such as compost rather than turning it over. During planting, soil is moved aside, creating a planting hole just large enough to accommodate garden additions.

When you feed your garden or homescape with compost, you're feeding it carbon! Compost is the magic ingredient for speeding up the soil-building process and returning excess atmospheric carbon to soil. It also protects soil structure, regulates soil temperature, and improves the water-holding capacity of soil, which, in turn, reduces erosion, decreases flood events, and improves water quality.

Remember the carbon cycle? Living roots provide a steady flow of carbohydrates and other, fundamental organic compounds such as amino acids in the form of exudates to soil microbes in exchange for hard-to-find nutrients and water. Basically, planting perennials and maintaining other year-round plantings such as ground covers provide a reliable food source for soil microbes and aid in protecting and cultivating soil structure. Plant roots, like those of trees and other deep-rooting perennials, help create deposits of stable soil carbon at depths reaching far below the upper soil horizons.

We can foster biodiversity by caring for the soil and growing a diverse range of plants. Include natives and perennials in your plant list, and remember that a biodiverse set of plantings fosters biodiversity of living organisms both above and below the ground.

Organic growing ensures the protection, health, and vigor of the systems upon which we all depend. For instance, use a diversity of plants to manage pests and apply nature-made compost once or twice a year to increase soil organic matter and fertility. Synthetic fertilizers, pesticides, and herbicides break the bonds of essential relationships within ecosystems, ultimately killing the natural system, including essential microbes. Synthetic fertilizers are also significant contributors of greenhouse gas emissions.

Finally, regenerative gardening provides a framework to do more good. With respect to growing and the environment, we're asked to contribute to the solution, rewild, and protect wild places, which are essential reservoirs for biodiversity.

These, then, are the essentials of regenerative gardening:

Protect the underground superhighway with no-dig gardening. This single act helps protect soil structure and ensures that carbon is safely stored underground and not released back out to the atmosphere.

Mimic nature, feed microbes, protect soil, and speed up the natural soil-building process by adding compost and other organic-rich amendments to your home garden and cityscapes.

REGENERATIVE GARDENING ESSENTIALS

Step away from tilling and take a no-dig approach.

Feed and protect soil with compost and organic mulch.

Keep living roots in the ground with cover crops and perennials.

Foster biodiversity by growing diversity.

Grow organically and say no to synthetic fertilizers, pesticides, and herbicides.

Celebrate living things and not only do no harm but also do more good.

Organic growing ensures the health of the systems on which we all depend.

Practice organic growing techniques to welcome life and support the carbon cycle rather than creating a toxic soup with synthetic fertilizers and chemical sprays that eventually find their way into drinking water and our food systems.

Grow a diverse range of plants to provide a diverse range and size of living roots in soil. Plants directly influence soil biodiversity while supplying microbes with a reliable food source thanks to the carbohydrates and other nutrients exuded by their roots. Living roots also help prevent erosion.

Foster biodiversity with biodiversity. Plants and insects and soil collectively work together to support biodiversity.

Do more good is our Hippocratic oath as growers and protectors of our one and only Planet A. When we do this, we're automatically giving the surrounding ecosystem room to breathe, repair, and regenerate.

To put it all together, carbon is the building block of life, and we can add carbon to our gardens by adding organic matter such as compost and plants. When soil is cultivated with organic methods that include composting, planting perennials, covering ground, and practicing no-till gardening, soil quality improves and the amount of carbon stored in soil increases. Biodiversity then increases, too, thanks to the natural feedback loops between life above ground and in the soil.

REGENERATIVE GARDENING SIMPLIFIED

1 We add carbon (the building block of life) to our gardens by adding organic matter such as compost and plants. At the same time, covering soil protects it from erosion and structural damage.

2 Roots exude carbohydrates and nutrients into soil.

3 Mycorrhizal fungi in relationship with plant roots produce glomalin, which helps carbon turn into humus, creating stable soil carbon protected within soil aggregates.

4 The hyphae of mycorrhizal fungi, also coated in glomalin, extend plants' reach.

5 CO_2 enters the soil carbon pool via leaf litter, compost and mulch, root exudates, and mycorrhizal fungi. Soil organic matter gives soil its structure, fertility, and water-holding capacity.

6 Some carbon is emitted back into the atmosphere through soil respiration and decomposition.

7 Feedback loops between plants and insects, and between plants and soil organisms, foster biodiversity above and below the ground.

Regenerative gardening pairs our understanding of the carbon cycle and the role of biodiversity in actionable ways to restore soil and the environment through the process of growing.

The feedback loops between the soil ecosystem and life aboveground rely on the health of the soil and the microbes that inhabit it. Even hummingbirds like this one depend on healthy soil.

ABOVE: Here's another view of the garden across from Community Market Natural Foods in Santa Rosa, California. This riot of edibles was planted straight into a healthy layer of compost that was originally placed over otherwise lifeless soil. **RIGHT:** Crops grown in no-dig farms and gardens have been found to provide greater nutrition than crops produced in tilled systems.

THE NO-DIG APPROACH

No-dig growing is the simple process of planting without tilling or excessive digging, researched and popularized by British market gardener and garden writer Charles Dowding. Grow a garden without digging? It may seem counterintuitive. How could it possibly work? But if you think about it, no-dig (also known as no-till) growing is how nature grows itself.

Nature doesn't come with a rototiller but lets the plants and animals do the work of creating suitable growing conditions. Leaves and other bits of organic matter fall to the ground from surrounding plants. Plant roots extend into the soil, where they do the work of creating pore spaces along with worms and other animals such as moles and voles. When we follow nature's lead, we can do the same and grow a garden with less work and fewer weeds.

Weed seeds can lie dormant in soil for years, waiting for the perfect conditions to be unearthed and grow. Tilling and digging gives them this opportunity, bringing them toward the surface, closer to light and water. To put it in perspective, some studies have found as many as 130 million weed seeds per acre! The link between tilling and weed growth is huge. If you follow no-dig principles and simply cover soil with compost and other mulches, you reduce the opportunity for weeds to germinate while feeding the soil.

There's another big benefit of the no-dig process. It's been said that the next frontier in nutrition science lies underground, where roots, microbes, and soil intersect. It only makes sense—it's the microbes in soil that shuttle nutrients to plants; their

BENEFITS OF THE NO-DIG PROCESS

Minimizes weeds and weeding because no-dig gardening minimizes the conditions in which weeds germinate and grow.

Ensures carbon stored in soil stays underground.

Protects the soil ecosystem and the underground superhighway of roots, fungi, and other organisms.

Reduces the risk of compaction. With no-dig, soil structure is protected from the outset rather than beginning in a compromised state (as with digging or tilling).

Helps maintain soil moisture and decreases erosion and risk of flood events thanks to soil structure maintenance and increased organic matter.

Helps produce crops with greater nutrition.

Applying a layer of compost over garden beds protects soil from heavy rains; improves soil tilth, structure, and water-holding capacity thanks to increased organic matter; and helps modulate soil temperature while buffering soil pH.

presence is vital to healthy food and a healthy planet. Regenerative no-dig farms and gardens, rich in microbial life, have been found to produce crops with exponentially greater nutrition than crops grown in tilled systems.

GETTING STARTED WITH COMPOST

Did I mention compost? Compost is a nature-based solution for growing a thriving organic garden and regenerating communities. It's the key to sequestering carbon and also the best food for your garden. Think of it as the ultimate superfood or a buffet like you'd find at an all-inclusive resort. But this smorgasbord is stocked with bits of nature: things like potato peels, eggshells, bark, worm poop, and loads of microbes. It follows the life = life equation. Basically, it takes life to create life.

Compost vs. mulch: What's the difference? Mulch is any organic material, including compost, put on top of soil and around plants to feed soil, retain moisture, and manage weeds. Compost is a decomposed mix of organic materials.

This two-bin compost system designed by Leslie Bennett (principal and founder of Pine House Edible Gardens) and Holly Kuljian (landscape architect) returns green waste and kitchen scraps to a small residential garden as compost.

And it's easy to make and apply. Simply spread it out like a blanket over your growing beds.

You may have heard it said that if food waste were a country, it would be the third-largest emitter of greenhouse gases following China and the United States. It's genuinely astounding, if not embarrassing. When food waste ends up in the landfill where it's deprived of oxygen and the other conditions needed for decomposition, it generates methane, a greenhouse gas more potent than carbon dioxide. According to the Environmental Protection Agency (EPA), food waste makes up approximately 20 percent of all the rubbish in landfills in the United States. Add the 13 percent of rubbish generated by yard waste, do some quick mental math, and it's easy to understand how converting food waste and yard trimmings into compost for our home gardens and communities is one of the easiest, most accessible ways to address the climate crisis.

The process of making compost follows a basic recipe. Yet, unlike your mom's chocolate chip cookies, it's a process-driven formula that's always changing

WHAT COMPOST DOES FOR YOU AND YOUR GARDEN

Sequesters carbon.

Grows flavorful, healthy food.

Provides a perfectly balanced diet for your garden and the soil ecosystem.

Fosters resiliency.

Reduces your carbon footprint, especially when it's made at home or locally sourced.

Protects soil and soil structure.

Acts as a sponge, decreasing runoff while increasing the water-holding capacity of soil, so moisture is available as plants need it.

Keeps food waste out of landfills and closes the food-to-plate-to-soil loop.

depending on circumstances such as the weather and the ingredients in your compost pantry. Whatever you do, don't overthink or complicate the process. You're not feeding koalas but microbes designed to consume whatever you throw at them.

THE RIGHT COMPOST SYSTEM FOR YOU

The method you choose for making compost depends on a handful of factors: the amount of space you have, the types of compostable materials such as yard trimmings and food scraps you have at your fingertips, and the amount of compostables you generate.

Larger spaces with the opportunity for a greater quantity of composting materials warrant larger composting systems such as tumblers, or single-bin or three-bin composters. In contrast, apartment living or patio gardening calls for more compact, multitasking, or community-run systems. No matter which compost system you choose, your best bet is to start with the simplest solution (remember the concept of parsimony) and plan to experiment and adapt your system as you go.

There's no need to add worms or other organisms to your compost pile. Once you begin piling up materials, the worms will follow. Basically: **if you build it, they will come**.

Cold composting is a set-it-and-forget-it method and will give you soil in nine months to a year. Hot composting takes a little more care and attention, but you can have finished compost from a hot system in a matter of weeks to a few short months.

COMPOST PILES

When making a traditional compost pile that's either freestanding or in a bin, work with a 3-by-3-foot or 4-by-4-foot area (1 to 1.5 meters on each side) and plan to create a stack that's taller than it is wide. If you plan to compost food scraps in an open bin system, I highly recommend enclosing it with ¼-inch mesh hardware cloth or a similar material to prevent rodents from becoming a problem. For those new to composting, it's a good idea to begin making your pile like layering a cake.

YOUR BASIC COMPOST RECIPE

The basic recipe for compost can seem kind of confusing at first. When you search for instructions on making compost, you get the age-old formula of 30 parts carbon, 1 part nitrogen, air, water, and microbes.

Don't let this fool you. The 30-to-1 carbon-to-nitrogen (C:N) rule of thumb is the balance of C:N that microbes need to cook up (or decompose) a compost pile and fast. In reality, it's a ratio that refers to the C:N ratio inside the plant matter you're mixing, not the amounts of matter you're mixing.

To put it another way, different organic materials have their own unique chemistry and varying proportions of carbon and nitrogen. For instance, coffee grounds have a C:N ratio of about 20:1, while wood chips are about 400:1. If you think about it too hard, the simple process of making compost can suddenly seem like a repeat of high school chemistry. Ahhh!

So how do you get the ratios of different organic materials to round out to a C:N ratio of 30:1? The answer is simple. You don't precisely, because getting it close is close enough. In reality, composting requires a basic formula with modifications along the way, much like making a pot of vegetable soup from scratch using mix-and-match ingredients from the garden. Whatever is fresh and ripe goes into the pot, no two recipes are alike, and some taste testing is required.

When combining materials, the best way to get it close enough is to mix 1 or 2 parts browns (carbon) to 1 part greens (nitrogen), add some activators (materials that jumpstart the composting process), water it enough to prevent it from drying out, stir it up to add air, and continue to stir once or twice (or not at all) while it cooks.

A note about grass clippings. While fresh grass clippings are an easy nitrogen source for your compost heap, they're also loaded with water. In fact, they're well over 50 percent water! They also tend to be reasonably uniform in size and shape so easily mat together, leaving very little air space. Combine these factors, and an otherwise good pile overloaded with grass clippings can quickly become slimy, smelly, and anaerobic. To avoid this, mix grass clippings with other ingredients before tossing them into the pile, or be sure to spread them out in a thin layer.

RIGHT: Rotting fruit, grass clippings, and green garden trimmings (often referred to as green waste) are excellent green materials. Grass clippings are rich in nitrogen and are highly effective compost activators, while twigs and branches are an important source of carbon or brown materials. You can mix browns and greens before adding them to a compost heap.

Compost bins like this one built by the organization LA Compost and its founder, Michael Martinez, can be found throughout the greater Los Angeles metro area. In 2019, LA Compost diverted 480,136 pounds of food and yard scraps from the landfill and created incredible soil for gardens and city landscapes. (It smells as good as it looks.)

You'll then develop a sense of the proportions and how your compost ingredients work together. Once you get the hang of it, you'll most likely find you're mixing your ingredients from the very start because you've developed a sense for what works best.

To get started:

- Chop up coarse materials to create more surface area. This will help shorten the composting period.
- Begin by placing the coarsest browns such as woody debris, twigs, and leaves on the bottom.
- Next add a layer of greens and then a layer of browns, and so on.
- Put any weedy or otherwise questionable plants in the middle. The middle is also a good place for food scraps.
- Vary the size and shape of materials to create air pockets.
- Avoid adding meats, fish, oils, oily food, dairy products, heavily coated or colored paper, walnuts (because their chemical makeup inhibits the growth of other plants), anything that could potentially be contaminated or filled with harmful chemicals, cat or dog poop, bread products.
- Get the layers nice and wet as you go, but don't drown them. Think of a rung-out dishcloth (not a kiddie pool) and aim for that.
- Continue adding your layers as you have them.
- Cover your heap with a tarp to help trap heat, speed the composting process, and protect your pile from weather events such as excessive rain.

For **hot compost**, plan to stir your pile or use a system that aerates the pile naturally. There's no hard-and-fast rule for how often to stir a pile. The frequency depends on the nature of the ingredients, outdoor temperatures, and how quickly you'd like your compost to finish. In general, the idea is that aeration speeds up the process because it adds oxygen to the system. However, moving things around can also slow the process because you could be exposing an otherwise warm

COMPOSTING MADE EASY

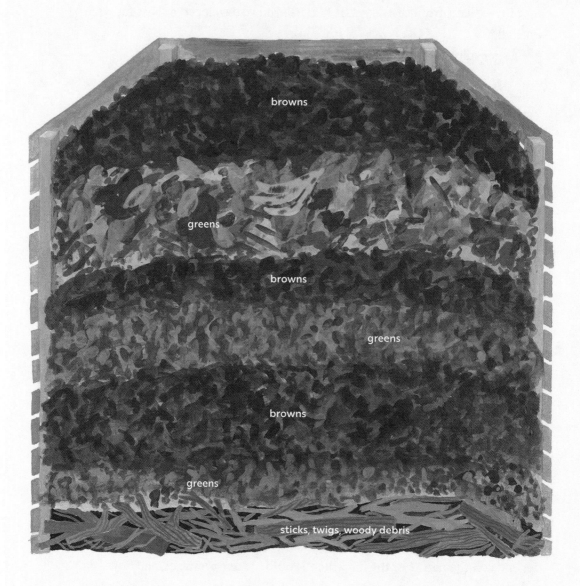

The compost pile you're aiming for alternates green (nitrogen-rich) and brown (carbon-rich) materials in layers, like a cake.

environment to cooler temperatures. Besides aeration, mixing a pile also helps move less-composted materials from the outside in.

For **cold compost**, you can set it and forget it. Think of this as an add-as-you-go pile. The rate at which it ages depends on the nature of the materials and the season. Don't risk adding weed seeds to cold compost piles. The chance of spreading them around your garden isn't worth it.

Check the pile periodically for any possible problems that need troubleshooting and continue adding moisture. Touch it and give it a good look. Rich, chocolatey brown compost is generally just right. If it's black or near black and smelly, it's most likely overly wet. If it's dull in color and dry to the touch, you'll need to add water and stir.

A compost thermometer is a great way to find out what's happening within your pile, even when you're cold composting. A good general temperature range to aim for when making hot compost is 130 to 160 degrees F (54 to 71 degrees C). In this range, weed seeds are sterilized, especially if your pile reaches at least 145 degrees F (63 degrees C) for about two weeks, yet it's also not too hot for beneficial microbes to thrive.

Once compost is finished, it needs to cure. Let it sit for several weeks or longer, and make sure it doesn't dry out and stays aerated.

WHAT TO PUT IN YOUR COMPOST PILE

Brown materials (carbon)

dry leaves

dry grass

woody debris such as bark or wood shavings

straw or hay

shredded paper and cardboard

pine needles

nutshells

corn stalks and husks

wood ash (considered either green or brown)

soil

twigs

Green materials (nitrogen)

green leaves

green plant trimmings

fruit and veggie scraps (don't forget the mash left over in your juicer)

coffee grounds

tea leaves and tea bags (if compostable and not made with plastic)

crushed eggshells

rotted manures such as chicken manure

wood ash (considered either green or brown)

rinsed seaweed

weeds (remove flowers and seed heads from plants like dandelions and thistles)

Compost activators

handful of garden soil

mature, active, or warm compost

comfrey

herbs

grass clippings

manure

alfalfa hay

Tumblers fit in a small space and make aerating easy.

TUMBLERS

Composting in tumblers may be the system for you if you're tight on space and prefer the ease of aerating the mix by tumbling rather than turning it with a fork. Because it's a closed system by design, it's also a sure way to recycle kitchen scraps without encouraging a rodent infestation. Dual compartment tumblers are practical because you can continue adding materials to one side while the other side, already filled, can simply be turned while it cooks.

To use a tumbler, fill it with a 1:1 or 2:1 mixture of browns to greens as if you're making a compost pile. Use the same troubleshooting techniques as with a traditional compost pile. Once the tumbler is full, stop adding materials and simply tumble it occasionally and add water as necessary. You'll know it's finished cooking when your food scraps and green waste have transformed into a rich, earthy material.

LEFT: Trimmings from the garden are perfect additions to any compost system. **ABOVE:** You can bury your food scraps directly in the garden.

GREEN WASTE BINS

If you're looking for a way to recycle green waste from your yard and house plants in a dedicated system (no food scraps), a green waste bin is the ticket. A green waste bin is an excellent system if you have a large yard and lots of trimmings. It's a perfect complement to a food scrap composting system like a worm bin or small tumbler. To use a green waste bin, simply toss in plant trimmings, weeds, leaves, and grass clippings as they're produced. You can eventually use composted materials at the bottom of the heap as mulch throughout your growing space.

IN SITU COMPOSTING

In situ is a fancy word for on-site. Why not skip all the fuss and toss your kitchen scraps straight into the garden? It's 100 percent possible. You can simply bury food scraps in the garden or run them through a blender first and then pour them over your garden (though you'll need a powerful blender).

There are also gardening systems that combine garden beds with in situ composting, like a keyhole garden bed. A keyhole garden is a circular raised garden bed with a keyhole-shaped indentation where the gardener can stand to add kitchen scraps to a composting basket. Microbes and worms decompose the scraps where the compost is readily available to your garden plants. You can make your own keyhole garden or find one commercially made.

VERMICOMPOST

Some of the best garden partners are worms, and for good reason. Worms are decomposing all-stars. They shred through organic matter as they move through soil and poop it out as a slow-release fertilizer, commonly referred to as vermicompost or worm castings.

Make your worm bin with plastic or wood tubs, or look for one that's premade and fits your space. Worm bins made of wood breathe well and are ideal, but they're also heavy and require an outdoor home. For indoor environments, bins made from plastic are standard and generally work well with generous ventilation. Like most living things, worms need air to survive. Worm bins with multiple tiers work best because they allow worms to move between levels and away from moisture accumulating in the bottom of the bin. Place your worm bin out of direct sun and in an environment that ranges from about 50 to 75 degrees F (10 to 24 degrees C).

Red wiggler worms are the best for home worm bins. Look for mail-order worms raised in your area so they don't have to travel far. One to two days in the

---

WHAT TO FEED YOUR WORMS

This	*Not this*
organic fruit and vegetable scraps	highly acidic foods such as citrus
crushed eggshells	pineapple or papaya (both high in digestive enzymes)
unbleached paper products	
hydrated coconut coir (especially when you plan to be away)	dairy
	oils and fats
teabags made from natural materials	salty foods
coffee grounds	meat products
unbleached, compostable coffee filters	processed foods
leaves	

CLASSIC WORM BIN COMPOSTING SYSTEM

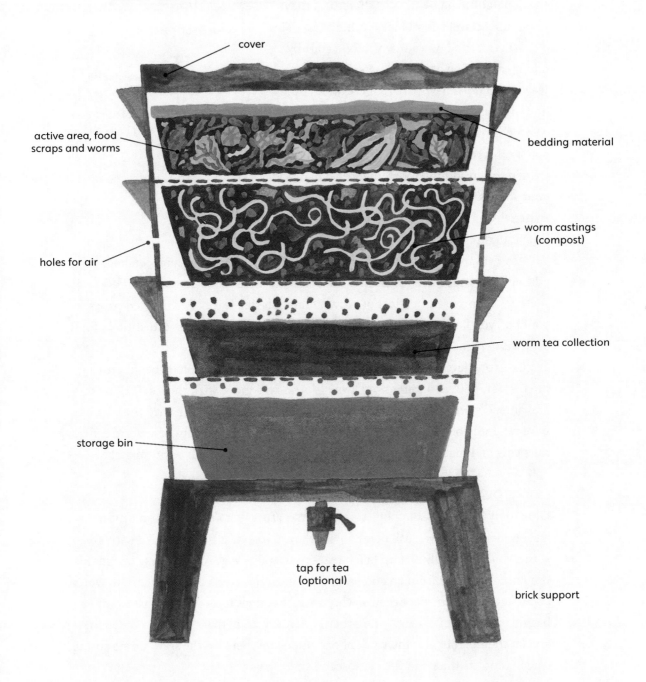

cover

active area, food scraps and worms

bedding material

holes for air

worm castings (compost)

worm tea collection

storage bin

tap for tea (optional)

brick support

mail is about all they can take. Also, it may be that a neighbor has worms to share, and they can simply travel a few blocks rather than miles.

When setting up your worm bin, start by adding a bedding of brown materials such as leaves, shredded newspaper, or coconut coir, and then spray it down with water. Like with a compost pile, it should feel like a wrung-out sponge. Next, I always throw in a handful of garden soil to add microbes and grit. Then, add your worms, cover them with more bedding material, and spray it down again so the bedding is damp.

After your worms have spent a few days in their new home, you can begin adding food scraps to a single tier. Cover freshly added food scraps with bedding material. If you're adding lots of brown materials like leaves or shredded paper to your bin, you'll need to spray it down with water. Otherwise, the moisture in food scraps is generally enough to maintain a damp environment.

Once one level is full and the composting process is complete, begin putting kitchen scraps in another empty level. Worms will move with the food. Harvest and amend your garden with the castings from the finished tier once the worms have migrated out. Think of the liquid that forms at the bottom of a worm bin as nutrient- and microbe-rich tea and feed it to your garden as it accumulates.

LEAF MOLD

Old moldy leaves are soil food straight from nature. If your yard doesn't produce an abundance of leaves, ask neighbors if they have extras to share. Like with green waste, you can simply pile up fallen leaves and walk away. And because leaf mold is commonly made from an abundance of autumn leaves, you don't have to worry about keeping them wet because winter weather does it for you. So instead of bagging up your leaves and piling them up by the curb, make a pile in your yard and let the microbes do the work of decomposing them on the spot. Come spring, spread it out as mulch in your landscape and garden.

Pile up leaves and let microbes turn them into compost.

LAY THE GROUNDWORK

MY FIRST TOOLKIT WAS AN AVOCADO GREEN METAL TACKLE BOX.
It was filled with everything my dad thought I'd need for success: two-tone red-and-white bobbers, weights, lures of different sizes, and fishing line. He knew that if I maybe caught a fish (or at least ended a day of fishing not too discouraged) and came home tired and happy, I'd most likely want to go back another day.

However, even with all the right tackle, it was up to me to learn the ways of the water and the habits of the fish, and to wait patiently. This is where my personal toolkit came into play—the one I didn't realize I was acquiring yet took with me wherever I went. It was growing slowly and steadily with experience.

Locate **soil testing labs** near you by calling the nearest university extension or horticulture society, or searching online for private soil testing labs. Request recommendations of certified organic amendments when submitting samples.

We form all kinds of toolkits across the timelines of our lives, like our nature quotient. It's our starting point for growing a successful garden or at least ending each day spent learning the ways of plants and the animals that visit feeling happy and far from discouraged but filled with hope.

Whether you're starting a new garden or improving one already planted, observation is one of the tools you'll reach for most often. What is your climate,

LEFT: My community garden plot provides a welcome place to plant and grow. **RIGHT:** Sometimes growing in raised beds is the easiest way to cultivate healthy soil and protect your garden from animals like gophers or ground squirrels.

and what are your frost dates? What type of soil do you have to work with? What's needed to cultivate healthier soil? How much light is available and how will you water what you grow?

Following observation, you'll need a quiver of problem-solving skills. Are raised beds, boxes, or containers best for you? Will you plant in the ground? Or work with a combination of options? If you have a plot of earth, spare edges along walkways, or borders that need filling, growing in the ground makes perfect sense. Inground plantings also allow you to jump into the carbon cycle with two feet.

PLANNING WHERE YOU'LL GROW

Start by looking close to home. What outdoor space do you have right out your door? Proximity and accessibility are equally important, making regular forays into your garden effortless and enjoyable. However, it might also be that the best place to grow is on a stairwell or deck, in a hellstrip, or in the places currently occupied by lawn. Or, if space is limited, it could be that borrowing a planting area from friends or a community garden is your best bet.

Choosing a site isn't just about the quantity of space available but also the quality of the area. For instance, what kind of light do you have? Are you working with sun, part sun, or shade? While many plants thrive in shade and part shade, most of our favorite food crops thrive best in full sun.

Knowing your soil leads to success. What is the soil type? Are you working with sandy clay, sandy clay loam, or straight-up clay? What are the available nutrients and pH? Does the soil contain toxins like asbestos, petroleum, or lead? It's helpful to send soil in for testing to provide a starting point as well as a benchmark for future comparison. You can perform a soil test with a home test kit, but I recommend sending it to a lab the first time around, especially if you're concerned about possible contaminants or adjusting pH before beginning the planting process.

You know that narrow, often unused area between the sidewalk and the curb? It's commonly referred to as a **hellstrip** because it's generally left to its own devices and occupied by turfgrass or unruly weeds. Just think of the positive impact if these spaces were dedicated to plants for people and wildlife!

This parking lot garden popped up in my neighborhood shortly after the beginning of the COVID-19 pandemic.

ABOVE: Why not grow a garden in the spaces along your sidewalk or in the hellstrip between the sidewalk and the street? **RIGHT:** Borage, a favorite of honeybees, grows in a hellstrip garden.

Consider the role of **topography and structures**. *Topography* refers to the contour and features of the land. Basically, the shape of the land can create wind tunnels, cold sinks, and banana belts. The best place for your garden may be a nice

big flat open area, but if this same area is at the bottom of a hill, it could also be a cold sink that controls your microclimate. Basically, cold air tends to sink and warm air rises. If you live at the bottom of a hill or in a valley, you may experience cold sinks. If you live along a ridge or high on a hill, your land may be warmer than surrounding lower areas. In many cases, topography also dictates aspect and therefore the path of available sunlight.

Cat's garden in pocket of radiant heat on the east side of her house grows the best tomatoes.

Structures such as buildings and trees in and near planting areas add another degree of impact, for better or worse. For instance, protected areas near buildings can trap warmth, making it possible to grow heat-loving crops like tomatoes and cucumbers in spaces that would otherwise be a challenge. Equally, trees can block available light and shift the direction and flow of wind.

At first glance, the placement of my friend Cat's garden seems counterintuitive. It's located on the east side of the house, and she lives in a coastal community that's reliably foggy in the summer months of July and August. Yet, she grows the

HOW MUCH SUN IS FULL SUN?

Full sun is six to eight hours of direct light a day. These hours can be contiguous or divided.

Part sun and part shade are three to six hours of sun a day. Plants that prefer part shade typically grow best with direct morning light and protected from afternoon sun, which tends to be the most intense light throughout a day.

Shade or full shade is three hours or less of direct sunlight a day.

Artist and landscape designer Todd Lynch of Ecotropy has tucked his personal garden into a gently rolling landscape near a barn and adjacent wooded area. It serves as a refuge for both people and wildlife. Lynch says he is "convinced that human well-being and ecological systems are interdependent."

best tomatoes! With cool, cloudy conditions during prime tomato-growing season, the assumption is that the best exposure is to the south or southwest. She gets around this by growing her garden between the protective shelter of the house and the neighbor's fence, where it benefits from a pocket of radiant heat.

PREPARING GROUND FOR NO-DIG PLANTING

The basic idea of no-dig growing is to amend the site rather than dig it up. A no-dig approach is ideal even for clay soil, but not all clay soils are created equal. If you're just getting started and have a hardpan of clay or severely compromised clay, it can help to give the area a one-time forking to improve aeration. (A basic pitchfork does the job.) If you're beginning with clay soil that's highly

RETHINKING LAWNS

I enjoy a good game of croquet as much as the next person, but how much lawn do any of us really need? Keeping this in mind, your lawn could be the very best place to plant your garden. You could ditch it altogether, converting it into a food and pollinator haven, or leave just enough to spread out a blanket and look up at the stars.

Here are some truths about lawns:

- Approximately 40 million acres across the United States are dedicated to turfgrass. This is an area larger than the state of Georgia and three times larger than any irrigated food crop! Now consider what that means for the rest of the globe.

- In the US alone, some 80 million pounds of mostly lab-produced, petroleum-based fertilizers and pesticides go into maintaining lawns.

- According to the EPA, 40 to 60 percent of nitrogen-rich fertilizers applied to lawns end up in waterways and groundwater, where they negatively impact plant and animal life and overall water quality.

- Synthetic fertilizers are costly to the climate from start to finish. An average of 4 to 6 tons of carbon ends up in the atmosphere for every ton of nitrogen fertilizer manufactured, not counting the emissions associated with packaging and transportation.

- Many of the tools used to maintain lawns—to mow and edge them—are fossil fuel dependent. Even most electric alternatives require the burning of fossil fuels unless the grid you draw power from relies on renewable energy. According to the EPA, 4 percent of total carbon emissions in the US are due to small gas-powered tools.

- To top it off, most lawns are food deserts—places where there's typically little to no forage for hungry pollinators, birds, and other wildlife.

TOP: If you must keep your lawn, maintain enough to create paths that can be mown and cultivated into living systems rather than covered with hardscaping. This is what Pam Karlson has done in her Chicago garden. **MIDDLE AND BOTTOM:** Pam lets clovers and other plants generally considered weeds thrive in the portions of lawn remaining in her backyard garden. These are an essential food source for wildlife such as bunnies and migratory birds.

Kelsey Adams at West Lane Flowers in Winooski, Vermont, grows her cutting garden with no-dig, regenerative organic principles. Note the wood chip paths and planting rows dressed with compost and straw.

compromised or perplexing, check with your local university extension office to learn more about the soil specific to your region along with tried-and-true recommendations for your area.

To begin preparing a new planting area, start by surveying your plot. Is it weedy or relatively bare?

If your planting area is bare, simply top it with 2 to 4 inches (5 to 10 centimeters) of compost. The depth of compost depends on your soil type and what you plan to grow. If your soil is predominantly clay or sand, add more compost to boost the overall concentration of organic matter. If it's in between and looks and feels like a decent mix of loam, a 2-inch layer of compost is most likely a sufficient starting point. It's also important to remember that food crops are typically hungrier and require more nutrition than flowering perennials or native plants. So if you're growing food, plan on 2 or more inches of compost, and if you're growing nonfood plants, plan on 2 inches or less.

compost, 2–4 in (5–10 cm)

one layer of cardboard or four sheets of newspaper

optional compost, 1–2 in (2.5–5 cm)

weeds or lawn, cut short

existing soil

IMPROVE SOIL WITH SHEET MULCHING

Kelsey Adams works in her no-dig, regenerative flower farm, where locally sourced wood chips, straw, and garden trimmings feed the soil and the flowers she so thoughtfully arranges for her clients and community.

TO USE OR NOT TO USE WOOD CHIPS?

You may hear some people say that wood chips rob the soil of nitrogen. This isn't completely true, but it's not entirely untrue either. Wood chips are inherently high in carbon. If we think of it in terms of composting, we know that microbes need a balanced diet of carbon and nitrogen for the decomposition process. Too much carbon, and microbes go in search of nitrogen to work things out metabolically.

According to the Cornell compost chemistry lab, a 30:1 carbon-to-nitrogen ratio is best. Wood chips can have a carbon-to-nitrogen ratio of 400:1. Fresh wood chips have the broadest range of nutrition, mainly when bark and leaves are in the mix. And while nitrogen near the surface may get tied up during the initial decomposition process of newly applied wood chips, this nitrogen doesn't go away. Rather, it's stored in the bodies of soil microbes, where it eventually cycles back into the soil system. That said, wood chips are, again, best applied to walkways and around plants similar to those that the wood chips originated from—plants such as woody perennials, shrubs, and trees—to reduce the risk of plants and microbes competing for available soil nitrogen.

Compost and mulch can often be used interchangeably, but the general rule of thumb is to apply organic matter composed of materials similar to those produced by that same landscape. So if you're feeding a food garden, use compost made from kitchen scraps and garden trimmings. If you're feeding a grove of trees or a perennial border, use wood chips or other woody debris and green waste. Leaf mold, shredded leaves, worm castings, and other homemade or locally sourced materials are also valuable.

If your planting area is covered in weeds or you're converting lawn to garden, first cut the weeds or lawn short. You can then apply a 1-to-2-inch (2.5-to-5-centimeter) blanket of compost (however, this is optional). Next, place a single layer of cardboard or four sheets of newspaper over the planting area. Spray it down with water, and top it with 2 to 4 inches (5 to 10 centimeters) of compost. This is known as **sheet mulching**. If you'd like to skip the use of cardboard or newspaper, apply a thicker layer of compost—4 to 6 inches (10 to 15 centimeters) is usually enough for an initial smothering of weeds.

Be mindful of the texture of the compost. Seeds and small seedlings have a much easier time rooting and taking hold in finer compost, so set aside finer compost for the uppermost layer and place the coarse compost in lower layers. Plan to reapply compost each spring and fall for continued soil building and long-term care.

Walkways can also be covered with cardboard and mulch. Apply materials such as wood chips to manage weeds, build organic matter, and bolster soil's carbon-storing capacity. If using wood chips, apply it 2 to 6 inches (5 to 15 centimeters) deep for best results.

RAISED GARDEN BEDS AND BOXES

You can also practice no-dig growing in raised garden boxes. Think of raised boxes as a clean slate. The no-dig process is simplified from the beginning because you're creating a soil environment from scratch in a bed or box resting on top of existing soil.

Veggie boxes in the Sonoma Garden Park community garden in Sonoma, California, are ringed with wood chip paths and mulched with straw, green waste, and other organic materials. Sonoma Garden Park is a city-owned park and demonstration garden managed by Sonoma Ecology Center.

Beds and boxes can be built or bought in all sorts of shapes and sizes and are appropriate for a wide array of sites. They help focus your attention, defining what to care for and where to plant. Raised garden boxes also solve common challenges like marauding gophers and poorly draining or contaminated soil. They're back savers too, eliminating time spent bending over or kneeling.

RAISED BED DESIGN

Typically, garden boxes are built from wood, bricks, or metal. They can also be constructed with straw bales, fallen logs, wattle fencing, or reclaimed materials. Design the box length and shape to fit the space. Just remember that longer boxes require reinforcing supports at their centers so they don't buckle and bow. Other design considerations:

- You should be able to reach the middle from either side. Generally, a box 3 to 4 feet (1 to 1.2 meters) wide is just right.

- The depth of beds is a reflection of what you plan to grow. Plants like lettuces, radishes, and herbs are okay with 12 inches (30 centimeters) of rooting depth. Tomatoes and other deeper-rooting plants are best grown in boxes 18 inches (46 centimeters) deep or deeper. But perhaps countertop-height boxes are best for you, to minimize bending over.
- Line boxes with gopher wire or ¼-inch mesh hardware cloth before filling with soil to prevent burrowing animals like voles, ground squirrels, and gophers from invading your garden from below.

FILLING RAISED BEDS

Once the logistics of size and shape are sorted out, you can get on with the business of creating a garden system. This is where your NQ (nature quotient) and regenerative gardening principles come back into play. Your goal is to create an environment inside your containers, raised beds, or boxes very much like the environment in the ground where a healthy soil system has room to develop. What's important to remember is that the larger the container, the easier it is to mimic a healthy soil system. This system then does much of the work of caring for your garden. Conversely, as containers, bins, and boxes shrink in size, they need more help from us.

The traditional rule of thumb for filling raised beds is to use an organic blend of 50 percent topsoil and 50 percent compost. If you go this route, look for soil makers in your region that deliver in bulk and offer certified organic mixes. If bulk soil isn't an option, it's possible to buy bagged planting mixes and compost, and combine them at home (but then there is the issue of plastic). What's imperative is to avoid mixtures containing peat moss and to buy hyperlocally.

Peat moss is a vital, nonrenewable resource. Peat moss can take up to a thousand years to grow 1 meter (a little more than 1 yard) deep. Peat bogs are carbon-storing ecosystems that provide homes to rare plants and animals. They also help filter and purify the air and water that moves through them. When peat is excavated, greenhouse gases are released into the environment. Pollutants and heavy metals such as mercury that have been captured over time through the bog's natural processes are also released, finding their way back into the greater ecosystem and waterways.

TOP: Boxes can be designed with low sides to simply hold soil in place, or much deeper to raise the height of beds to sitting or countertop height. This edible landscape was designed by Leslie Bennett and Holly Kuljian.
ABOVE: Large containers like stock tanks work well for gardening on a deck or patio.

My friend Lisa Barringer built garden boxes to suit her hillside garden, placing them to optimize sun while keeping them as close to the kitchen as possible. Lisa's cat, Yeti, enjoys the warmth of the garden's stepping-stones.

Garden boxes don't all have to be boxes. Todd Lynch of Ecotropy created raised beds in his Massachusetts vegetable garden with Corten steel to suit his space and aesthetic.

But let's rethink this traditional rule of thumb, because one of the biggest issues with gardening in elevated boxes or bins is that the topsoil has to come from somewhere. Even if it's local, it's a resource (and living system) removed from its point of origin and transported elsewhere. Keeping this in mind, the better, more carbon-friendly solution is to pair a mix of locally made compost with other organic materials to fill your beds. Hügelkultur and lasagna gardening are similar methods for doing this.

Approximately 2.2 million tons of **leaves** went into US landfills in 2017, about 25 percent of the total 8.7 million tons of yard waste filling dumps that year.

Hügelkultur is a technique long used in Eastern Europe and Germany for creating mounded planting beds by composting in place. Organic matter such as compost, leaves, grass cuttings, straw, and kitchen scraps is layered onto cut-up logs, sticks, and twigs. While it may initially seem like a lot of work, adapting hügelkultur for filling boxes is worth it. The process creates incredibly well-draining soil that retains moisture, ultimately producing a rich, fertile, airy growing medium.

Make hügelkultur beds with materials sourced on-site or within your community to decrease transportation and increase closed-system recycling of what would otherwise be green waste. The trick is to save the finest compost for the upper layers so you can plant smaller starts and seeds right away.

A hügelkultur-style garden bed in Sonoma Garden Park recycles what would otherwise be green waste.

Lasagna gardening is very similar: layers of organic matter piled up one on top of another. When these layers decompose, they create organic-rich soil for your garden so you don't have to import it from off-site. Because it's basically a compost pile that's generating heat, it's generally warmer than the surrounding soil, so you can plant it sooner in spring. Lasagna gardening also gives you the freedom to plant intensively, placing plants closer together and in greater abundance due to the soil's richness.

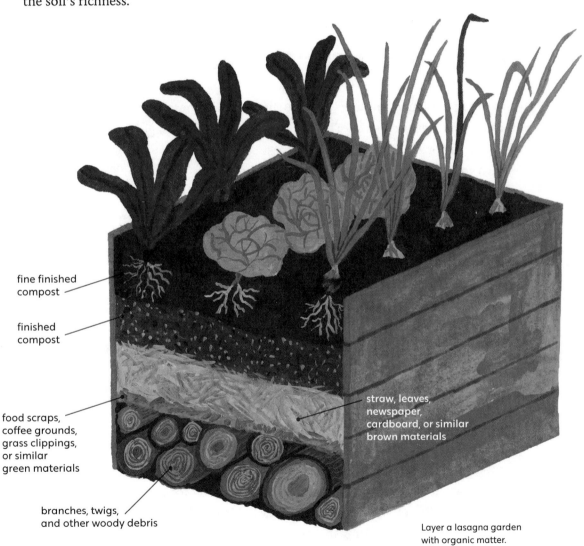

fine finished compost

finished compost

food scraps, coffee grounds, grass clippings, or similar green materials

branches, twigs, and other woody debris

straw, leaves, newspaper, cardboard, or similar brown materials

Layer a lasagna garden with organic matter.

For successful lasagna gardening:

- Avoid adding treated wood, redwood, cedar, eucalyptus, or walnut to the pile.
- Water the layers as they're created.
- Top off the last layer with a healthy blanket of finished compost so you can begin planting right away.

FILLING SMALL CONTAINERS

Two of the primary concerns when growing in small containers are soil compaction and nutrient depletion. That's why using a soil mix designed for containers such as an organic potting soil is your best bet when you're filling small containers for the first time. It helps slow the inevitable compaction process inherent in small containers while maintaining aeration and a place for nutrient uptake.

Aeration refers to the air spaces in soil. A soil with good aeration allows for an exchange of water and oxygen necessary for both roots and microbes within the spaces between soil particles.

Potting mixes are lightweight and designed to drain well while holding moisture. Look for potting mixes that are organic and free of peat, containing peat substitutes like coconut fiber or coir. If you can't find one, you can mix some up with a few basic ingredients.

PLANNING WHAT YOU'LL GROW

Just as important as planning *where* you'll grow is thinking about *what* you'll grow. Have dreams of a cupboard chock full of jars of homegrown, homemade tomato sauce, salsa, and jam? Or enough frozen berries for winter-long smoothies, enough dried fruit for your child's lunches and baking? This is when bumper crops from focused plantings come into play. Let the ingredients you'll need guide you

MATERIALS FOR FILLING AND AMENDING GARDEN BEDS AND BOXES

Leaves Collect them from your yard or neighborhood. If you're using leaves as a mulch, consider shredding them first with your push mower to speed the decomposition process. Be sure to avoid leaves from trees such as black walnut, which contain chemicals that deter the growth of other plants.

Worm castings, also known as worm poop or vermicompost. Add them to all your plantings to increase disease resistance, resiliency, and available nutrients. Fill new boxes with 10 percent or more worm castings for best results.

Composted manure Chicken and cow manure are both excellent. Wherever you get your manure, be sure it's from a trusted source or buy certified organic. If the manure is from animals raised in environments where herbicides are used, chances are these same herbicides will end up in your garden, where they'll continue to act as a weed killer, compromising your food plants, flowers, and soil. It's also important to make sure the manure is well composted; if it's too green, it can burn plant roots.

Straw An inherently carbon-rich amendment, straw can be applied as a mulch or paired with green materials and added into beds when they're first made. Look for seedless, locally grown straw whenever possible. In California, I reach for rice straw because it's a by-product of the rice industry and if seeds are present, they don't overrun my garden with unwanted grasses as is typical with oat straw. If you're in an area that receives consistent year-round rain or you have problems with slugs, you may want to avoid mulching with straw, because it's a welcome hiding place for slugs and snails.

Biochar A form of charcoal, biochar is made by cooking down organic materials such as yard waste into a state of pure carbon that when charged with nutrient-rich amendments and added to garden soils improves moisture and nutrient retention. Charge biochar by mixing it in with your compost pile or by soaking it in a mixture of chlorine-free water (if your city water has chlorine, simply let it sit out for a few days so the chlorine evaporates) and nutrient-rich ingredients such as worm castings, liquid seaweed, or compost tea. Biochar provides a number of benefits, including increasing the water-holding capacity of soil, which means you can water your garden less. It also facilitates plants' ability to take up nutrients.

Use organic potting soil in small containers to address soil compaction and nutrient depletion.

MAKE YOUR OWN PEAT-FREE POTTING MIX

2 parts coconut coir

1 part organic compost

1 part rice hulls

Rice hulls are a carbon-rich, sustainable substitute for perlite. Look for them at landscape supply stores or ask your garden center to order them for you.

Experiment with this basic recipe by adding ingredients such as worm castings, charged biochar, coarse sand, and fir bark.

When considering what to grow, start with the plants you love.

KNOW YOUR HARDINESS ZONE

Hardiness zones, initially developed by the US Department of Agriculture, have been adopted in various forms worldwide. Use your hardiness zone as a guidepost for understanding how well various plants might withstand the lowest average winter temperatures in your area, and avoid planting anything with a minimum hardiness zone rating higher than yours. For example, if you live in hardiness zone 6 and you're considering a plant with a specified hardiness range of zones 7 to 9, it may struggle and fail to thrive.

Hardiness zone maps are available for much of the world. To find yours, start at plant-maps.com. When you know your hardiness zone, you can select plants to grow that are rated at that number or lower.

It's important to note that hardiness zones don't consider conditions such as heat tolerance, humidity, rainfall, freeze and thaw cycles, climates with cold summer nights like in high desert regions, and microclimates. Also, the zones in which a particular plant species is hardy can vary depending on the specific variety or cultivar.

in the planning process. For instance, if it's pickles you're after, plan to grow a pickle garden with garlic, dill, cucumbers, and extra pole beans. If it's salsa you crave, tomatillos, tomatoes, peppers, garlic, and cilantro might make your planting list.

Begin the plant selection process with a basic set of questions.

- What are the plants you love? These may be plants you love to cook and eat, plants from your childhood that hold unforgettable memories, or plants you've come to love over the years.
- What would you like your planting area to do? Or, put another way, what's its purpose? Think multiservice. Most plants fulfill a variety of roles. For instance, some can be grown to create privacy or to cook and eat while also feeding pollinators and keeping living roots in the ground.

David Grist of Burlington, Vermont, designs gardens for biodiversity and resilience.

- What are your growing conditions? What is your climate, which hardiness zone do you live in, and what are your average frost dates? Are you working with full sun, part sun, or shade? Also, what's your soil type? These conditions help define what you can grow and temper your love list.

PLANTS FOR PEOPLE AND THE PLANET

THOUGHTFUL PLANTING captains the journey of writing a story that's close to home, one in which pen and paper are traded for seed and soil. The plot line is for you to choose, and the narrative is one that adheres to the central theme of form follows function. Essentially, the shape your garden takes from concept to planting is a direct function of its purpose and your vision for the space. It's also an extension of your story and the story of the landscape in which you live.

Believe it or not, **store-bought asparagus** is among the top producers of greenhouse gas emissions. It racks up the food miles when flown from Latin America, where it's commonly grown. If you're an asparagus lover, look for locally grown or grow it at home.

The ultimate goal is to choose plants based on the role they play in your everyday life as well as for their biodiversity-driving, climate-mitigating abilities. For instance, perennials reliably cultivate the soil ecosystem at varying depths, while plants like natives are essential for supporting wildlife. Are you growing food with companion plants? Would you like to plant a border for pollinators or perhaps a meadow? Maybe you're looking to fill a handful of containers with plants that provide the biggest impact for both the kitchen and bees?

The plant lists in this chapter are designed to be used as a guide to jump-start the planting process. They're not complete but a place to begin. Because your region and growing space are unique to you, some of the plants referenced here may or may not be a perfect fit. However, you might find plants within the same genus or family that are well matched to your site and meet your needs.

TRADITIONAL EDIBLE PERENNIALS

"Plant once, harvest forever." This is a saying you'll often hear when it comes to traditional perennial vegetables like these. And it's true. Edible perennials once planted can be harvested season after season with minimal care. Yet, in reality, this is a group of heavy lifters. They're tried and true in both the garden and the kitchen. I'll never forget my first taste of garden-grown sorrel and its profusion of flavor. The tangy leaves readily transform simple dishes such as salads and soups. Or lovage! When do you ever find lovage at the market? Edible

Artichokes growing in Anita Rackerby's garden. If well mulched, artichokes are perennial down to USDA hardiness zone 6 and warmer.

Sunchoke tubers are packed with nutrition, though you could simply grow the plants for their summer and fall blooms.

perennials are also an excellent addition to the garden because they maintain living roots in the ground that ultimately feed soil microbes in exchange for water and hard-to-find nutrients, collectively building soil carbon stores.

Artichoke (*Cynara scolymus*) Grow artichokes for their edible flower buds or their blooms. Zones 6–7 and warmer.

Asparagus (*Asparagus officinalis*) Enjoy up to six weeks of harvesting every spring once plants are mature. Zones 3–10.

Chives (*Allium schoenoprasum*) Among the first garden edibles to flower in spring, chives hold up through continual harvesting and winter storage. Zones 3–10.

Jerusalem artichoke or sunchoke (*Helianthus tuberosus*) I find it's best to plant sunchokes in containers or otherwise unused areas because they quickly multiply and take over. Zones 3–9.

Lovage (*Levisticum officinale*) Its leaves can be used much like parsley. Add it to salads and soups, eat the root as a vegetable, and use the seeds as a fennel-like spice. Zones 4 and warmer.

Edible perennials like rhubarb (growing near the spigot in this photo) can be planted directly in the ground.

Purple tree collard or tree kale (*Brassica oleracea* var. *acephala*) Tree collards provide an easy, regular supply of hearty leaves and take well to propagating if growing as an annual. Zones 7 and warmer.

Radicchio (*Cichorium intybus*) Bold and bitter, this is an easy-to-grow leafy vegetable to expand your palate. Zones 4 and warmer.

Rhubarb (*Rheum rhabarbarum*) A harbinger of spring, rhubarb grows best in regions with long winter cold spells. Zones 3–8 though up to 10 in certain areas.

Sorrel (*Rumex acetone*) Its tangy leaves are as good in salads as they are in soups. Zones 4–9.

EDIBLE FOREST GARDEN PERENNIALS

If you'd like to mimic nature in the process of growing your garden, a forest garden could be the perfect planting strategy to explore. Also called an edible food forest, a forest garden aims to create a functioning forest system by incorporating a productive orchard, woodland, and kitchen garden while optimizing the various forest layers from the floor to the canopy.

Good-King-Henry (*Blitum bonus-henricus*) This is an easy-to-grow spinach substitute. Zones 3–9.

Ostrich fern grows (with Solomon's seal) in Eric Toensmeier's garden.

Ostrich fern (*Matteuccia struthiopteris*) Native to North America, this fern produces edible fiddleheads in spring and reliable, summer-long foliage. Zones 2–8.

Ramps or wild leeks (*Allium tricoccum*) Native to eastern North America, ramps are garlicky and wonderfully pungent. Grow them in shady, moist areas. Zones 3–7/8.

Sea kale (*Crambe maritima*) Sea kale is halophytic, meaning it's tolerant of salty soil and water. All parts of the plant are edible, from the roots to the shoots, tender leaves, and blooms. Zones 4-8.

Watercress (*Nasturtium officinale*) Grow it as an aquatic perennial and for its superfood powers. It's one of the most nutrient-rich foods, loaded with vitamin K and other vital compounds for health and longevity. Zones 6–10.

Grape vines growing in Sonoma Garden Park, Sonoma, California.

ABOVE: This runner bean tunnel supports the vines while providing an area of interest in the garden **RIGHT:** Passion fruit is very nutritious, and the vine offers a number of opportunities in the garden. Consider placing it to provide privacy and where you can easily enjoy its blooms.

EDIBLE PERENNIAL VINES

Vines are enthusiastic growers, often climbing the heights of telephone poles and winding their way around buildings. They're also capable of outcompeting and even smothering essential native plants. It's always smart to triple cross-check before planting vines to be sure you're choosing the right plant for the right place.

Chayote (*Sechium edule*) A member of the gourd family, this is an edible perennial that can be prepared much like squash and eaten fresh or cooked. Zones 7–11.

Fuzzy kiwi (*Actinidia deliciosa*) Both the leaves and fruit are fuzzy. Grow in pairs of male and female plants. Zones 7–9.

Grapes (*Vitis* species) Grape hardiness depends on the variety. Don't be shy with winter pruning, as proper pruning is critical for healthy plants and fruitful harvests. Zones 4–10.

You'll need **two kiwi plants**, a male and a female, for successful fruiting with most varieties, because most are dioecious (plants produce either male or female flowers and are not self-fertile). ***Actinidia arguta*** 'Issai', however, is a self-fertile variety from Japan that can be grown as an individual.

Hardy kiwi (*Actinidia arguta*) The degree of hardiness and minimum number of chill hours that kiwis require depend on the variety. 'Issai' doesn't require a mate. Zones 3–10.

Maypop (*Passiflora incarnata*) This is a cold-tolerant cousin of *Passiflora edulis*. Zones 6–11.

Passion fruit (*Passiflora edulis*) This vine has gorgeous flowers and incredibly healthy fruits filled with antioxidants, iron, and B vitamins. Zones 9b–11.

Scarlet runner beans (*Phaseolus coccineus*) While this bean needs generous winter mulching in colder climates for successful perennial growth, it can also be grown as an annual. Zones 6–11 or colder with generous mulching.

PERENNIAL HERBS

Most plants are multitaskers and provide a variety of services. For instance, many herbs double as companion plants to kitchen garden edibles. Fragrant herbs can confuse pests, making it harder for plant-eating insects to find their preferred lunch spots. Many herbs and other food garden plants also provide season-long blooms to support pollinators.

Anise hyssop (*Agastache foeniculum*) While considered a short-lived perennial, it's not reliably so. Be prepared for enthusiastic volunteers and a parade of visiting pollinators. Zones 4–9.

Epazote (*Dysphania ambrosioides*) Commonly used in Mexican dishes, this is an aromatic short-lived perennial herb that can become weedy due to self-seeding. Zones 4–12.

Fennel (*Foeniculum vulgare*) Best grown in garden beds, where it's easiest to manage. Plants can become invasive in certain regions. Zones 6–10.

French tarragon (*Artemisia dracunculus* var. *sativa*) Grow it for its peppery, anise-like flavor and give it some protection if growing in zone 2. Zones 2/3–9.

Lavender (*Lavandula* species) Like many of the others, this herb doubles as a companion and landscape plant. Zones 5–9/10.

TENDER HERBS

basil 'Mrs. Burns' Lemon'

basil 'Cinnamon'
black cumin
borage
calendula

chervil
cilantro 'Dwarf Lemon'
cilantro 'Slo-Bolt'
cumin
dill 'Greensleeves'
flat-leaf parsley
Florence fennel
German chamomile 'Zloty Lan'
holy basil

Lemon balm (*Melissa officinalis*) Lemon balm is in the same family as oregano, thyme, and mint and shares many of the same spreading growth habits. Zones 4–9.

Marjoram and oregano (*Origanum* species) These are pollinator favorites that spread very much like mint, so observe caution when planting. Zones 4–10.

Mint (*Mentha* species) Mint hardiness depends on the mint variety, but no matter which ones you grow, be sure to plant them in containers, or they'll easily spread throughout your garden. Zones 3–11.

Pineapple sage (*Salvia elegans*) While not as hardy as some of its cousins, pineapple sage is a versatile plant and adored by hummingbirds. Zones 8–11.

Roman or English chamomile (*Chamaemelum nobile*) This is a true chamomile with feathery leaves, a creeping habit, and small white blooms. Zones 4–11.

Rosemary (*Rosmarinus officinalis*) According to researchers studying communities with high rates of centenarians, using rosemary liberally in cooking could be vital to living one hundred years or more. Zones 8–11.

Sage (*Salvia officinalis*) I love this culinary herb because it holds its own in the landscape, providing excellent structure in a perennial border, plus bees love it. Zones 5–10.

Salad burnet (*Sanguisorba minor*) Mild-tasting, this herb likes some shade and is easy to tuck in between other plants. Zones 4–8.

Thyme (*Thymus vulgaris*) One of my favorite hardy herbs, thyme is beloved by pollinators and infuses everyday cooking with incomparable flavor. Zones 5–10.

TOP: Parsley tolerates partial shade and can be sheltered from summer sun by pairing it with taller kitchen garden edibles. **BOTTOM:** French tarragon, center, grows above sweet basil to its left and sorrel to its right.

TOP: Anise hyssop grows in my community garden plot. **BOTTOM:** Grow lavender in perennial borders or near a vegetable garden as a companion plant.

TOP: Mint flowers are a pollinator favorite. **BOTTOM:** Chamomile forms a spreading mat and blooms throughout the summer.

TOP: While not extremely cold hardy, pineapple sage is a welcome addition to a children's garden. Rub its leaves to release its pineapple-like aroma. It can also be grown for aromatherapy, cocktails, and tea.
BOTTOM: Grow rosemary outdoors as an annual in cold climates or plant it in a container and bring it indoors if you're in a hardiness zone below 8.

ANNUAL VEGETABLES AND FRUITS

Annual vegetables and fruits are kitchen garden mainstays. Look to this group for plants you can add to seasonal meals, preserves, and for daily grazing.

Broad beans (*Vicia faba*) Grow these beans, also known as fava beans, to cultivate and build tough soil—and you can eat the flowers, shoots, and pods.

Broccoli (*Brassica oleracea* var. *italica*) Broccoli is packed with vitamins, minerals, and important phytonutrients.

Brussels sprouts (*Brassica oleracea* var. *gemmifera*) Brussels sprouts are a significant source of vitamin K and calcium.

Cabbage (*Brassica oleracea* var. *capitata*) One of the largest cabbages ever grown weighed nearly 140 pounds (64 kilograms)! Start seeds indoors in winter to grow your own giant cabbage.

At its core, the practice of **companion planting** is designed to increase productivity and overall plant success through beneficial plant pairings. You can achieve companion planting with the commonsense approach of placing taller plants at the north or east side of beds, sun-loving plants to the south and west, and plants that need support near those that are sturdy such as sunflowers.

Cauliflower (*Brassica oleracea* var. *botrytis*) Cauliflower is tops on my list for summer-to-fall eating. If you buy it at the store, it's always wrapped in plastic. Grow your own for zero waste, seasonal flavor.

Corn (*Zea mays*) Consider growing your own three sisters garden, planting corn with beans and squash.

Cucamelons (*Melothria scabra*) Also known as Mexican sour gherkin or mouse melon, cucamelon is native to Mexico and Central America. It can be grown as a perennial in zones 7–11.

TOP: Cucamelons taste like slightly tangy cucumbers. **BOTTOM:** Broccoli is an excellent cool-season crop.

Cucumbers (*Cucumis sativus*) Like Brussels sprouts, cucumbers are high in vitamin K and other essential minerals.

Eggplant (*Solanum melongena*) Known as aubergine in parts of the world, eggplants are rich in antioxidants, high in fiber and minerals.

Ground cherries (*Physalis* species) You rarely see ground cherries, a warm-season fruit, in your local market, but once you begin growing them in your garden, you'll have plenty to share.

Hot peppers (*Capsicum* species) With so many different varieties to try, it's worth experimenting with unfamiliar selections each season if you live in a reasonably warm climate.

TOP: Summer squash, cucumbers, tomatoes, shishito peppers, and red onions are great annual vegetable choices. **BOTTOM:** Eat pole beans fresh off the vine or grow varieties best dried and cooked in soups and stews like 'Autumn Zebra' or black turtle beans.

Kohlrabi (*Brassica oleracea* Gongylodes Group)
Historically referred to as German turnip,
kohlrabi is technically a biennial vegetable
closely related to wild cabbage (however
much it looks like a spaceship).

Melons (*Cucumis* species) This is a broad group
of plants with a wide range of habits and
flavors. Grow melons to cover ground as well
as for the fruit.

Peas (*Pisum sativum*) Peas are an excellent
crop for cooler climates and, like pole beans,
are important soil builders.

Pole and bush beans (*Phaseolus coccineus*) Plants in the legume family like
pole beans provide nutrition to soil, wildlife, and people.

Potatoes (*Solanum tuberosum*) You can grow potatoes much like fava beans
to cultivate soil and prepare a new planting area. If it's calories you're
after, potatoes are among the best food crops to grow, pound for pound.

Summer squash (*Cucurbita pepo*) When you're tired of eating the fruit,
try the flowers. If your plants aren't fruiting, try cutting back some of
the leaves.

Tomatoes (*Solanum lycopersicum*) There are well over ten thousand
cultivars of tomatoes, plenty of varieties to try in every climate and region.

LEAFY GREENS

arugula
endive
kale
lettuce
mâche
Malabar spinach
mizuna
nasturtium
purslane
red leaf amaranth
sea kale
spinach
Swiss chard
tatsoi
tree collards
wild rocket
yukina savoy

TOP LEFT: Kale harvest; **TOP RIGHT:** Leaf lettuce mix; **CENTER LEFT:** Nasturtiums grow well both in the ground and in containers. **CENTER RIGHT:** Red leaf amaranth; **BOTTOM LEFT:** Swiss chard; **BOTTOM RIGHT:** Malabar spinach growing in my friend Lisa's garden catches the eye of her cat, Yeti.

TOP: Try growing a new-to-you squash like this Japanese kakai pumpkin. **BOTTOM:** 'Indigo Rose' tomatoes surprise with their unusual color.

ROOT VEGETABLES

One of the things I love about root vegetables is that many can be sown directly in the garden, allowing you to skip the steps of starting seeds indoors and then transplanting. Root vegetables are also easily interplanted to optimize space and can be sown successively for continual harvests.

Beets (*Beta vulgaris*) Ranging from earthy to sweet, beets are easy to grow from seed and packed with nutrition.

Carrots (*Daucus carota* var. *sativus*) Give them light soil and consider scatter sowing them or plant them in neat rows. Best grown with companion plants or in elevated beds to mitigate carrot flies.

Celeriac (*Apium graveolens* var. *rapaceum*) Also known as celery root, celeriac can be eaten freshly grated on salads, cooked and mashed like potatoes, or roasted.

Rainbow carrot blend

Garlic (*Allium sativum*) It's best to plant garlic in the fall and plan to store it for use through the warmer months after spring harvesting.

Onions (*Allium cepa*) Sow them successionally from seed or plant out sets for continual harvesting from garden to table.

Parsnips (*Pastinaca sativa*) Direct sow in spring for a fall to early winter harvest, and remember they're slow to germinate.

Cosmic Purple and Nantes carrots

LEFT: Bunching onion **RIGHT:** 'Cherry Belle' and 'French Breakfast' radishes

Radishes (*Raphanus sativus*) Try experimenting with unique varieties that you'd never find at the store, such as 'Black Spanish Round' or 'Candela Di Fuoco'.

Rutabagas (*Brassica napobrassica*) In spring, direct sow for fall harvesting, or in warm climates plant in fall for a spring harvest. Let rutabaga mature into the colder months for the best flavor.

Salsify, black (*Scorzonera hispanica*) and white (*Tragopogon porrifolius*) These cousins produce uniquely long taproots with an equally unique flavor that resembles oysters or artichokes.

Turnips (*Brassica rapa*) Some of my favorites are salad turnips such as 'Tokyo Market' and 'Hinona Kabu'. Don't forget to eat the greens, because they're as good as the roots.

TOP LEFT: Calendula and borage pair well in the garden. Grow them for the edible flowers and for their benefits as companion plants. **TOP RIGHT:** Nasturtiums add color and a peppery flavor to salads. **ABOVE:** Oregano blooms are a favorite of bees and can be added to vinegars and salads or used as a garnish. **CENTER LEFT:** Violas are perfect border plants in the veggie garden, filling in where needed and covering ground, as well as offering edible blossoms. **LEFT:** Nigella and chamomile both have edible flowers.

PLANTS WITH EDIBLE FLOWERS

anise hyssop	chives	nigella
arugula	cornflower	pea
basil	dill	radish
borage	fennel	rose
broad bean	garlic	rosemary
calendula	honeysuckle	squash
chamomile	lavender	thyme
cilantro	mint	viola
chervil	nasturtium	

Use caution when eating foods like edible flowers for the first time. It's important to know what you're eating before you eat it. Positively identify plants or plant parts and ensure they're organic. If you have pollen allergies, know that flowers contain pollen and may be problematic. Begin with small amounts of new foods like edible flowers and wild plants.

BERRIES

Berries are nutritious and easy to grow, and they offer seasonal grazing in a range of unique and sometimes hard-to-find varieties. Growing your own also means you can avoid the unnecessary plastic packaging commonly found at the store.

Berries with prickly stems—blackberry, raspberry, marionberry, loganberry, boysenberry (*Rubus* species) Be prepared for their rambling, spreading nature. Look for thornless varieties and consider growing them in containers or with root barriers. Zones 3 and up, depending on the variety.

Blueberries (*Vaccinium corymbosum*) Blueberries prefer acidic soil, like full sun but will take some afternoon shade in hot climates, and offer year-round interest in the garden. Zones 3–11.

TOP: Raspberries are among the easiest berries to grow at home, producing prolific crops. Choose from varieties with different maturation times. **BOTTOM LEFT:** Blackberries, like other *Rubus* species, ramble and spread. **BOTTOM RIGHT:** Blueberries are ornamental as well as nutrient dense, adding fall color to the garden.

LEFT: Currants can be sweet or tart. RIGHT: Alpine strawberry (*Fragaria vesca*) grows naturally throughout North America.

Currants and gooseberries (*Ribes* species) Many of the cousins in this genus can take some shade and offer both sweet and tart berries. Look for species native to your region. Zones 3 and up.

Goji berries (*Lycium barbarum*) Also known as wolfberry, goji berry is an easy-to-grow superfood. It likes well-drained soil with a pH between 6.8 and 8.1. Hardy to zone 5.

Honeyberries (*Lonicera caerulea* var. *edulis*) Sweet like their name implies, honeyberries are worth growing for their flavor and versatility. They thrive in soil with a wide pH range of 5 to 8 and require two different varieties to produce fruit. Zones 3–10.

Strawberries (*Fragaria* species) Try experimenting with different cultivars. Grow in the kitchen garden, on a patio in containers, or in the landscape. Zones 5 and up, depending on the variety.

Apple trees come in a range of growth habits.

FRUIT TREES AND SHRUBS

It's possible to espalier fruit trees like citrus, apple, pear, and fig and grow them in compact forms to create a wall or living fence, or to line a path.

Apple (*Malus domestica*) This is a highly diverse group with many different cultivars of varying growth habits. Look for dwarf rootstock and consider espalier trees for small spaces. Includes crabapples. Zones 3–9.

Chestnut (*Castanea* species) These are gorgeous trees that produce edible nuts encased in a prickly outer skin. Zones 4–9.

Citrus—lemon, lime, orange, grapefruit, tangerine, mandarin, kumquat (*Citrus* species) Most are sensitive to freezing temperatures, and some grow well indoors. Zones 8–11.

Citrus trees can be espaliered against a bare wall to save space, create interest, and benefit from the warmer microclimate.

Fig (*Ficus carica*) In the same family as mulberry and breadfruit, this is a unique and wonderful plant with hardy and less hardy cultivars. Zones 5–11.

Medlar (*Mespilus germanica*) Medlars are fall to winter bearing with fruits that taste much like apple butter. They can be grown as shrubs. Zones 4–9.

The fruit of the medlar tastes like apple butter.

Mulberry (*Morus* species) A fast-growing tree producing berrylike fruits, mulberry is a favorite of birds, and its fruit can be made into jam, wine, and tea. Be cautious with white mulberry as it's considered invasive in many parts of the world. Zones 4–8.

Peaches and plums are both classified as stone fruit.

Pawpaw (*Asimina triloba*) Native to eastern North America, the pawpaw is a small tree that produces a sweet, tropical-tasting fruit. Zones 5–8/9.

Pear (*Pyrus* species) Prized by cider makers and bakers, pears are rewarding to grow. Consider growing a unique cultivar that you otherwise wouldn't find at your grocery store. Zones 4–9.

Persimmon (*Diospyros* species) *Diospyros virginiana* is an eastern North American native. 'Fuyu' is excellent for eating and appealing to the eye. Hardiness depends on variety.

The pawpaw is seeing a comeback in popularity because it's hardy and disease resistant, and it produces highly nutritious fruit.

Pomegranate (*Punica granatum*) Technically a shrub, pomegranate can get fairly large (up to 30 feet tall) and is extremely tough. It's also ornamental and available in numerous cultivars. Zones 7–10.

Quince (*Cydonia oblonga*) A unique cousin to the apple, this is a tree with attractive blooms and tart fruit. Zones 4/5–9.

Stone fruit—apricot, cherry, nectarine, peach, plum, pluot (*Prunus* species) Choose the best variety for you based on your hardiness zone. Zones 4–9.

Walnut (*Juglans* species) Like chestnuts, these are attractive, durable trees producing edible nuts. Zones 4–9.

PLANTS FOR BUTTERFLIES

Butterflies (and moths) need both host and nectar plants. Host plants are the places where moths and butterflies lay their eggs and where the larvae (or caterpillars), once hatched, feed until transforming into adults. These are plants such as milkweed for monarchs, dill and fennel for swallowtail butterflies, and grasses for skipper butterflies.

When selecting plants for pollinators like these, it's essential to consider adding host plants as well as nectar plants and to remember that many are species specific, like monarchs with milkweeds. Also, consider some of the holes caterpillars chew in your plants' leaves as something to celebrate. It means your garden is an ecological haven, not just for butterflies but also for birds and other animals.

Bee balm (*Monarda* species) Bee balm and its cousin, coyote mint (*Monardella* species), are essential plants for butterflies, bees, and hummingbirds. Zones 2–10, depending on species.

Buckwheat (*Eriogonum* species) An important plant for both butterflies and bees. Native varieties are especially beneficial. Zones vary by species.

Coneflower (*Echinacea* species) This is a tough, attractive, and cold-hardy plant that's also water wise. Zones 3-9.

Joe Pye weed (*Eutrochium* species) Native to the eastern and central regions of North America, Joe Pye weed prefers growing in wet conditions and is tolerant of sun or shade. Zones 3/4–9.

Echinacea tolerates drought and neglect.

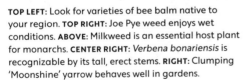

TOP LEFT: Look for varieties of bee balm native to your region. **TOP RIGHT:** Joe Pye weed enjoys wet conditions. **ABOVE:** Milkweed is an essential host plant for monarchs. **CENTER RIGHT:** *Verbena bonariensis* is recognizable by its tall, erect stems. **RIGHT:** Clumping 'Moonshine' yarrow behaves well in gardens.

ABOVE: Sunflowers provide a platform for pollinators like bees to land on.
RIGHT: Single dahlias are wonderful in bouquets.

Mexican sunflower (*Tithonia rotundifolia*) and other aster family plants with a similar shape These are typically grown from seed as annuals and are great companions in the veggie garden. Zones 10–11.

Milkweed (*Asclepias* species) Milkweed species native to your region are the best way to support migrating monarchs. They act as both a host plant for monarchs and an important nectar source for a long list of insects and pollinators. Zones vary by species.

Phlox (*Phlox* species) Many are early spring bloomers, and while some grow quite tall, others are terrific as ground covers. Zones 4–8/9.

Sage (*Salvia* species) This wide-ranging group includes ornamentals and culinary herbs. Zones vary by species.

Verbena (*Verbena* species) Verbena species are found throughout the world, and they vary in shape and size. One of my favorites is *Verbena bonariensis*. Zones vary by species.

Yarrow (*Achillea* species) Look for clumping varieties like 'Moonshine' for tidy gardens and spreading types for meadows. Zones 3–9.

SOME OF THE BEST BEE-FRIENDLY PLANTS

agastache
allium
aster
basil 'African Blue'
berries
borage
calendula
catmint
comfrey
currant
dahlia, single-flowered

foxglove
fruit trees
heather
lavender
oregano
penstemon

rosemary
sage
scabiosa
sunflowers
thyme
verbena
yarrow

BIRD FAVORITES

Remember our baby chickadees in the first chapter? The best plants to grow for birds are ones that provide shelter and a food source of berries, seeds, or insects—with native plants being the all-stars. According to Douglas Tallamy, professor of entomology and author of *Nature's Best Hope*, native oak trees support more than 550 species of butterflies and moths. (Compare this to the 5 species supported by nonnative ginkgo trees.) Insects like these and their caterpillars are a critical source of food for birds. That said, don't discount the benefits of your kitchen garden filled with companion plants; loads of feasting can be done there, too (including your vulnerable and tasty newly planted starts).

Aster (*Symphyotrichum* species) Often the last to bloom in fall, asters are a reliable source of seeds. Zones vary by species.

Buttonbush (*Cephalanthus* species) *Cephalanthus occidentalis* is native to North America in the East and the South and is a bird favorite. Zones vary by species.

Common mullein (*Verbascum thapsus*) and ornamental cultivars Introduced to Australia and North America, mullein is native to Asia, Africa, and Europe. It's a source of seeds and a host to numerous insects. Zones 3–9.

Hedgerows of native plantings, such as sage and California fuchsia, ring the flower beds at Bluma Flower Farm on a rooftop in Berkeley, California, and create an oasis of forage and habitat for birds.

Pam Karlson, garden designer and artist, calls this hawthorn her bird tree. It's a focal point in her garden and provides important forage and cover for migratory birds.

Asters provide a seed buffet for birds.

Dogwood (*Cornus* species) Dogwoods are generally small to medium-sized trees with showy blooms and berries. Look for a species native to your region. Zones vary by species.

Elderberry (*Sambucus* species) Elderberries are important to insects and birds and produce berries from spring to fall, depending on the region and the species. Zones vary by species.

Hawthorn (*Crataegus* species) Birds such as warblers, loggerhead shrikes, waxwings, and robins visit and nest in hawthorns. Zones 5–9.

Honeysuckle (*Lonicera* species) This is a beautiful vine, though often susceptible to aphids. Look for a species native to your region. Zones 4–9.

Liatris (*Liatris* species) The tall spikes of liatris blooms provide forage for birds and pollinators such as butterflies and pair well in perennial borders. Zones 3–9.

TOP: Liatris bloom spikes draw butterflies and birds. **BOTTOM:** The hips on this rugosa rose are favored by thrushes and waxwings.

Zinnia

PLANTS TO ATTRACT HUMMINGBIRDS

agastache
bee balm
bleeding heart
catmint
columbine
currant
delphinium
epilobium
flowering quince
honeysuckle
liatris
lilac
lily
lobelia
lupine

mimulus

penstemon
phlox
sage
zinnia

Marigold (*Tagetes* species) A common go-to companion plant, marigold adds a layer of diversity and a source for seeds. Most are annuals.

Oak (*Quercus* species) Oaks provide food and shelter to many different animals. Bees, butterflies, moths, squirrels, deer, songbirds, turkeys, and cavity-nesting birds such as owls and wood ducks are among its many visitors. Zones vary by species.

Roses, shrub and wild (*Rosa rugosa, R. canina, R. californica*) Rose hips are a food source for birds such as thrushes and waxwings. Zones 4 and up.

Sunflower (*Helianthus* species) Sunflowers are generous seeders and are available in a range of shapes and sizes. Most are annuals, but some like *H. angustifolius* are perennial. Zones vary by species.

Teasel (*Dipsacus* species) Goldfinches, grosbeaks, and buntings visit teasel from autumn to winter. Zones vary by species.

Viburnum (*Viburnum* species) Sometimes called snowball bush, viburnum is a host plant to numerous butterflies, and its berries are a favorite of birds. Zones 2–9.

Virginia creeper (*Parthenocissus* species) This native North American vine, much like ivy in Europe, is an important food source for birds, insects, and other wildlife. It provides berries in fall and winter. Zones 3–9/10.

SOIL-BUILDING PLANTS

It turns out that many of the plants vital for wildlife are also excellent at building and improving soil fertility. Countless plants actively fix nitrogen, transforming nitrogen gas into an organic, soluble form just right for plants, and others help cultivate soil through their ability to form extensive root systems even in the toughest soil. Some are beneficial because they can be cut back extensively and quickly rebound, growing more vigorously with each pruning. Use these for green mulching or what is often referred to as "chop and drop." This plant group includes alfalfa, bush indigo, comfrey, nettles, the Siberian pea tree, and cover crops like clover, peas, vetch, and other legumes. Six easy-to-grow cover crops are listed here to get you started.

Annual ryegrass (*Lolium multiform*) Plant it in the spring or fall, and be sure to cut it back before seed heads form to prevent unwanted spreading. The timing of planting depends on the climate. Zones 2–9.

Broad beans (*Vicia faba*) While broad beans (also called fava beans) don't spread to cover soil, they do an excellent job of breaking up tough soil and preparing it for planting in consecutive seasons. Cool-season annual.

LEFT: Purple clover is an attractive cover crop, especially to bees. **RIGHT:** Kelsey Adams of West Lane Flowers has put the dandelion greens she's just weeded back onto the bed, where they'll compost in place while acting as a green mulch.

Buckwheat (*Fagopyrum esculentum*) Best grown in the warm season, buckwheat covers ground and builds soil while its flowers are a nectar source for pollinators such as honeybees and other beneficial insects such as hoverflies. It's grown as an annual.

Clover (*Trifolium* species) Plant it to fix nitrogen, build soil, cover ground, and support insects. The timing of planting depends on the variety. Zones vary by species.

Peas (*Pisum sativum* or *Pisum arvense*) Like clover, peas such as field peas and Austrian winter peas do an excellent job covering ground, fixing nitrogen, and providing flowers for bees and other pollinators. Annual.

Vetch (*Vicia* species) Another nitrogen fixer, vetch, is excellent for building and protecting soil. Avoid using the more aggressive vetch cousin commonly called crown vetch (*Securigera varia*) as a cover crop. It's grown as an annual.

EVERGREEN GROUND COVERS

ajuga
bearberry
candytuft
ceanothus (trailing)
creeping phlox
ferns
sedum
strawberries
thyme
violets
wild ginger

Stawberries keep the ground covered as they supply fruit.

Like cover crops, ground covers perform a wide range of services. They protect soil, decrease soil erosion, act as a living mulch, and suppress weed growth. They offer refuge for overwintering beneficial insects, and they also ensure a steady source of living roots. Living roots are vital for maintaining the plant and soil microbe partnership that helps drive the carbon cycle. All sorts of plants can be grown as ground covers, including strawberries, thyme, bunchgrasses, and phlox.

Compost activators are plants rich in nitrogen, or "greens" in composting lingo. These plants are easy to grow on-site to jump-start the composting process. For instance, dandelions make excellent compost, and offer other benefits as well. While dandelions are commonly considered noxious weeds, particularly in North America, they also provide early spring forage for bees and a range of health benefits for people. Dandelions are edible from tip to tail. Their bitter greens aid digestion and are an excellent source of vitamins A, C, K, and E.

EASY-TO-GROW COMPOST ACTIVATORS

borage
chamomile
clover
comfrey
dandelion greens
grass clippings
fennel
lovage
nettles
tansy
yarrow

Comfrey helps build soil and can be cut back as needed and added to compost. It pairs well with ornamentals like zinnias.

GROW AND GATHER

"EVERY SEED CONTAINS THE POTENTIAL TO SAVE THE WORLD," writes Bartholomew, Archbishop of Constantinople, in the book *Sacred Seed*, a collection of essays edited by the Global Peace Initiative of Women. Seeds are life-filled packages connecting each of us to the past and the future while firmly planting us in the present. They hold the promise of growth and restoration, and provide the tangible gifts of life, including the food that fills our plates and the fibers from which we make fabrics for our clothing and homes. In every seed is a tiny plant waiting to grow, but also an entire garden—or forest—because a single seed is the origin of many others.

How, then, do we grow anything from seed? Growth is a frame of mind and approach to life as much as it's an act. The tools needed to grow as a human, to foster healthy relationships, and to grow a garden or community, are the same. Start by paying attention. Remember that challenges are often good for you—they help keep your brain elastic and curious. Practice leads to deeper understanding and change, and immense learning is found in the lives (and gardens) of others. You may even discover that as you nurture your garden, it's in reality nurturing you.

GETTING TO KNOW YOUR PLANTS

The basic principles of growing food and flowers are the same. To begin, getting to know where a plant is from, no matter if it's edible or ornamental, will give you a head start on the growing process, as will knowing if you're working with annuals or perennials.

WHERE ARE YOU FROM?

Ask a plant where it's from, and there's a whole lot of learning in this initial exchange. The same is true with people. One of the most common questions asked when we meet someone for the first time is "Where are you from?"

Of course, a conversation with a plant is quite different from one with a human, but if a plant is native to Minnesota, the Mediterranean, or Mexico, the image that comes to mind with each is just as telling as with a human. These

HOW TO GROW

The surest way to grow anything—from plants to friendships to children—is to pay attention. In fact, much of what's needed to cultivate any healthy relationship is what's required to cultivate a thriving garden.

Growing begins with listening. **Listen with all your senses**—including your heart—and the plants will help lead the way, guiding you as to how to care for them and prepare them from garden to table.

Choose wisely. Just as you don't have to be everyone's friend, you don't have to grow every plant. Instead, grow the plants that are right for you, your climate, and your space. To effectively choose what to grow, you need to get to know your particular microclimate, available planting area, and growing conditions while keeping in mind the outcomes you'd like to achieve.

Accept your plants for who they are and your garden for what it is. This will reduce any possible future frustrations while increasing your overall success. For instance, growing sun-loving plants like tomatoes in the shade will only lead to defeat.

Make the most of fertile ground and, where it doesn't exist, cultivate it. Any good relationship begins with a solid foundation that's then cared for and fed.

Remember important dates. Think of the timeline of your garden much like the timeline of your life and the people with whom you share it. Add birthdays, anniversaries, frost dates, and what to plant when to your calendar.

Grow more of what's working and let go of what's not.

Whether you're growing squash or zinnias, the principles are the same. Get to know where a plant is from and what conditions it prefers.

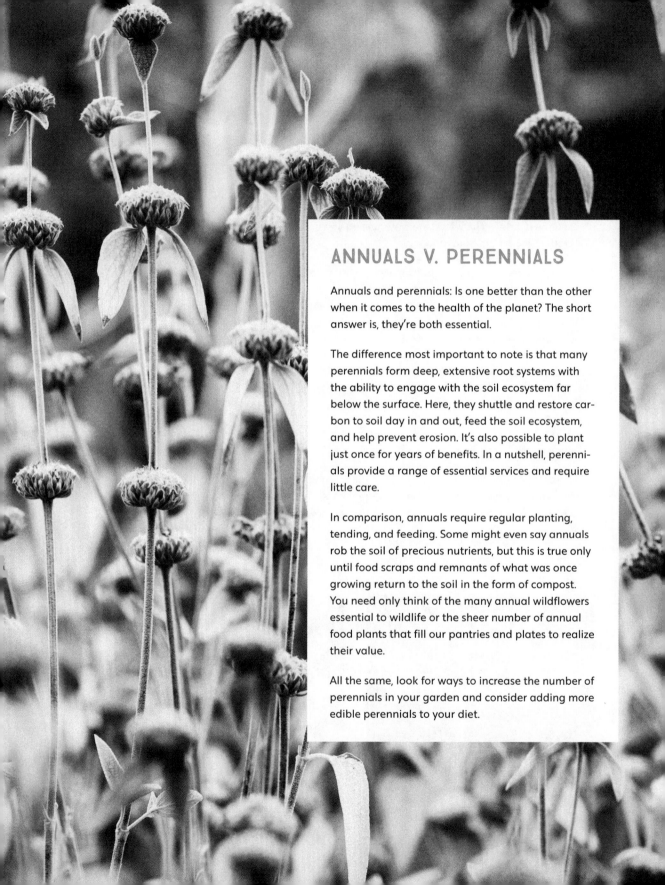

ANNUALS V. PERENNIALS

Annuals and perennials: Is one better than the other when it comes to the health of the planet? The short answer is, they're both essential.

The difference most important to note is that many perennials form deep, extensive root systems with the ability to engage with the soil ecosystem far below the surface. Here, they shuttle and restore carbon to soil day in and out, feed the soil ecosystem, and help prevent erosion. It's also possible to plant just once for years of benefits. In a nutshell, perennials provide a range of essential services and require little care.

In comparison, annuals require regular planting, tending, and feeding. Some might even say annuals rob the soil of precious nutrients, but this is true only until food scraps and remnants of what was once growing return to the soil in the form of compost. You need only think of the many annual wildflowers essential to wildlife or the sheer number of annual food plants that fill our pantries and plates to realize their value.

All the same, look for ways to increase the number of perennials in your garden and consider adding more edible perennials to your diet.

places frame home ground and the associated comfort range within which plants are happy to grow. Is it a dry-summer climate? Or are the summers warm, humid, and wet, punctuated by a growing season flanked with snow? Or is it a climate that's reasonably mild yet tending to warm and humid (if along the coast) or alpinelike (if in the mountains)?

ARE YOU AN ANNUAL OR A PERENNIAL?

Another question to ask is if a plant is an annual or a perennial. The thing to know for growing is that annuals and perennials have different survival strategies.

The strategy of an annual is to produce lots of seeds to ensure survival from season to season. So, if it's an annual, plan to grow it from seed or buy it as a start. However, many annuals such as basil can be regrown by simply rooting cuttings in water.

Perennials also produce seeds, but most have other, alternate strategies to ensure survival:

Annuals like these sunflowers make natural bird feeders when left out after flowering.

- creating daughter plants from stolons (like with strawberries)
- layering by setting roots from the ends of branches that have been buried (like with blackberries)
- cloning themselves into ever greater bunches (that can then be easily divided)
- sprouting clone plants from rhizomes (like with mint)
- regrowing from bits of themselves (like with soft wood, woody stems, or root cuttings)
- self-sowing with seeds

Allium 'Millenium' is an ornamental herbaceous perennial best grown from divisions or starts.

GROW YOUR WAY TO A SMALLER CARBON FOODPRINT

The way we grow and consume (or fail to consume) food is responsible for a large carbon foodprint. While agriculture is to blame for one-third of global greenhouse gas emissions, food waste post-production generates 8 percent of total emissions. In fact, approximately 30 percent of the food produced around the globe is wasted. Some of this waste occurs before food reaches the supermarket. And much of the rest goes from larder to landfill. Transporting food from field to market to home is another key greenhouse gas emitter, often referred to as food miles.

It's possible to eat your way to a trimmer carbon waistline by growing some of your own food, eating with the seasons, and shopping hyperlocally. Growing some of your own food is your leg up on reducing your carbon foodprint, especially if you grow your food using the nature-based solutions outlined in this book. You're less likely to waste food you've grown yourself. And if the food you grow doesn't all

The relative carbon emissions of food transport by ship, train, truck, and plane. While transport by boat generates the least emissions, the increased number of cargo ships traveling the world's oceans comes at a cost to marine life, notably as marine mammal collisions and pollution.

LEFT: Growing some of your own food goes a long way toward reducing your carbon foodprint. RIGHT: My daughter, Sinéad, helps in the community garden. My hope is that she'll form a deep appreciation of food and its origins.

make it onto your plate, it can easily go back into your garden using one of the composting techniques outlined earlier in the book.

Just as critical is eating with the seasons. Chances are the tomatoes grown locally but in hothouses out of season require more energy than tomatoes grown in a seasonally appropriate climate and transported across the globe to your supermarket.

Another issue related to food transport is nutrition. Fruits and vegetables are at the peak of nutrition at the point of harvest. The farther produce travels and the longer it's stored, the greater the nutrient loss. It can take five days for produce to travel from farm to market in the US, and then it often sits an additional one to three days at the market. It might then sit in your refrigerator for another week. That's nearly two weeks!

Produce that travels from one hemisphere to supply out-of-season markets in the other hemisphere is often picked unripe before its full nutritional value is realized. It then travels for several weeks in a refrigerated ship. Total nutrient loss and the resulting loss of flavor vary depending on harvesting and handling practices, travel duration, and storage methods during travel and at point of purchase. But the bottom line is that homegrown not only tastes better but is also more nutritious.

STARTING SEEDS

While many seeds can be sown directly in the garden, many benefit from being started indoors, where they're protected from foraging animals and kept warm. Get to know your frost dates and check seed packets to learn the best practices for the plants you're growing. Whether you're sowing straight in the ground or in containers, the process is very much the same.

Begin by smoothing the soil surface and ensuring the soil isn't too dry. (Water tends to roll right off bone-dry soil and can easily wash your seeds away.) Consider using a peat-free seed-starting mix when growing indoors. I often use a basic planting mix that's nothing fancy, with good success.

TOP LEFT: Many seeds can be sown directly in the garden. **TOP RIGHT:** Press larger seeds into the soil individually.
ABOVE LEFT: Soaker hoses are a good way to keep seedlings moist when seeds are direct sown in the garden.
ABOVE RIGHT: These newly emerged sprouts need lots of light.

CHEAT SHEET FOR EATING WITH THE SEASONS

What's in season in your region, and what can you grow to expand your food options and improve your nutrition? Also, what's unique to your corner of the world? As a native of Northern California, I still remember the first time I had fiddleheads, just harvested from the woods in New England and sautéed in butter with garlic and a pinch of salt. It's a dish I would struggle to grow in my mild coastal climate because the ferns they were gathered from prefer colder weather.

Use this guide to help you eat with the seasons and decrease your carbon foodprint. Note that seasonal availability depends on where you are in the world and your regional climate. Availability is also dictated by plant variety. For instance, everbearing strawberries generally have two harvest seasons, one in early summer and another in early fall, whereas June-bearing strawberries bear fruit in June, as their name implies.

TOP LEFT: Broccoli, carrots, and peas are reliable spring vegetables harvested from my friend Norma's garden.**ABOVE:** Shishito peppers are a heat-loving summer crop. **LEFT:** Kale is a cool-season vegetable that endures through the winter.

SPRING

These are often edible perennials, crops with short growing seasons, or plants started in winter and harvested in spring.

apricots (late spring, early summer)

artichokes

arugula

asparagus

blueberries (April to late September)

broad beans (also known as fava beans)

broccoli

carrots

cauliflower

cherries (late spring)

chives

cilantro

fiddleheads

green onions

lettuces

mangoes

mustard greens

onions

parsley

parsnips

peas

radishes

ramps

rhubarb

spinach

Swiss chard

SUMMER

Summer is the time for heat-loving crops, many of which have long growing seasons.

basil

berries

blueberries

carrots

cherries (early summer)

corn

cucumbers

dill

eggplant

figs

garlic

grapes

green beans

lettuces

melons

mint

okra

oregano

parsley

peppers

radishes

rosemary

sage

stone fruit (like peaches and plums)

summer squash (such as courgettes or zucchini)

thyme

tomatoes

AUTUMN

Sometimes you can squeeze in another round of cool-season veggies in fall while enjoying foods planted in summer that mature into fall.

apples

arugula

beets

Brussels sprouts

cabbage

carrots

chestnuts

cilantro

grapes

kale

lemons

lettuces

parsley

pears

persimmons

potatoes

sunchokes

sweet potatoes

winter squash (including pumpkins)

WINTER

Think cold-hardy crops and crops that store well.

beets

broccoli

Brussels sprouts

cabbage

carrots

celery

citrus

endive

escarole

kale and other hardy greens

kiwi

leeks

mâche

mushrooms

onions

pomegranate

potatoes

winter squash

AVERAGE ANNUAL FROST DATE BY HARDINESS ZONE

Zone	Average Last Spring Frost	Average First Fall Frost
Zone 1	June 1–June 30	July 1–July 31
Zone 2	May 1–May 31	August 1–August 31
Zone 3	May 1–May 31	September 1–September 30
Zone 4	May 1–May 31	September 1–September 30
Zone 5	March 30–April 30	September 30–October 30
Zone 6	March 30–April 30	September 30–October 30
Zone 7	March 30–April 30	September 30–October 30
Zone 8	February 28–March 30	October 30–November 30
Zone 9	January 30–February 28	November 30–December 30
Zone 10	January 30 or earlier	November 30–December 30
Zone 11	Frost free year-round	

There's more than one way to plant:

- Sprinkle seeds over the soil surface and then cover them with soil, pressing lightly to ensure good soil-to-seed contact.
- Use a pencil, chopstick, or finger to create a furrow at the planting depth best for your seeds (again, see the seed packet), and then cover them over with soil to make sure they have good soil-to-seed contact by pressing lightly.
- With larger seeds, you can press them into the soil individually, cover, and then press the soil down over them.

Label your plantings with the variety and date. Water using a watering can or a similar device with a gentle spray. If growing in small containers or paper pots, water them from the bottom in a tray.

Most seeds don't require light to germinate, but if you're growing them indoors, be sure they get lots of light as soon as you see sprouts emerge and plan to supplement with grow lights if ample sunlight isn't available. Generally, twelve to sixteen hours of sunshine a day is enough. If seedlings become tall and leggy, they need more light.

TRANSPLANTING SEEDLINGS

If you've started your seeds indoors and they're ready to go out, you first need to prepare the tiny plants for what would otherwise be a sudden change in climate. To do this, harden seedlings one day at a time, beginning the week before they're scheduled to go into the garden (as per your frost date calendar). On day one, put them outside for one to two hours and then add an hour each day for the week.

When watering newly transplanted seedlings and starts, using a solution of water and liquid seaweed can help **reduce root shock**.

When your seeds have grown into sturdy seedlings, it's time to plant them out. If they're tiny, hold them by the seed leaves and prick them out with a pencil or chopstick. To do this, simply tease them out from the bottom up, gently lifting the roots and surrounding soil. Then make a depression in their new home and tuck them in just as gently as when you pricked them out.

Gently tease out tiny seedlings with their roots and surrounding soil.

Slide larger starts out of their pots with roots and soil intact.

Starts grown in paper pots can be planted out as is. Bury so the roots are fully submerged in the soil.

If they're larger starts grown in containers, soil blocks, or paper pots, you can simply plant them out as is, making sure to bury them to the crown or base of the stem so the roots are fully submerged. With starts grown in containers, press or pound on the container's sides to release the plant and then slide it into your hand.

HOW TO PLANT IN A NO-DIG GARDEN

Whether you're growing in a raised bed or the ground, the process is the same: disturb the soil as little as possible and create a planting hole only as deep as needed to accommodate the roots of what you're planting.

For vegetable starts and seedlings, use a tool like a planting trowel, hori hori, dibbler, your hands, or even a chopstick (for the smallest of seedlings) to create a planting hole just big enough for the plant in question. Simply make your hole, tuck in your plant, cover the roots, and press your plant into place to ensure roots have good root-to-soil contact.

If you're transplanting herbaceous perennials, small shrubs like berries, or fruit trees, you'll need a larger tool like a spade. But, again, you're merely digging a hole large enough for the roots of the plant—no extra diameter needed because you're letting the soil ecosystem do the work.

TROUBLESHOOTING THE GROWING PROCESS

It's important to remember that plants are wired to grow and most often thrive when given the opportunity. However, there can be challenges when growing seeds and starts, and these usually boil down to one of several recurring themes.

What happens when your seeds don't sprout or seedlings wilt and die unexpectedly?

- If your seeds aren't sprouting, it could be you've given them too much water or not enough. Too much water will cause them to drown and rot, whereas not enough water interrupts the germination process.
- It could also be the temperature is all wrong. Most often, if the issue is temperature, it's not warm enough. However, some plants like lettuces won't germinate if it's too hot (85 degrees F—or 29 degrees C—or higher). Check your seed packets to understand the optimum temperature range for growth.

Plants growing in the right place need very little extra care and, in many cases, grow without any care once established.

- Sometimes seeds are planted too deep. Remember, there's a baby plant inside each seed, and to survive, it has to reach the soil surface.
- If seeds have been exposed to light, air, or water during storage, they may no longer be viable, and you need to start again with a fresh batch of seeds.
- If you notice seedlings are wilting at the stem, damping-off is most likely your problem. Damping-off is caused by overly wet conditions and inadequate air circulation that ultimately encourages the growth of certain naturally occurring soil fungi and bacteria. To treat, simply

cut back on watering, give your seedlings plenty of air, and sprinkle a little cinnamon on the soil surface near the base of the stem. If this doesn't work, start over and consider using a peat-free soilless mix.

How do you know if your plants are getting the nutrition they need?

Plants that appear discolored or out of the ordinary may need fertilizing. Begin with compost or a tea made of compost, manure, or comfrey, as described later in the chapter. Consider a balanced slow-release fertilizer when growing in containers.

How much water is enough?

Good question! The answer is, it depends. The amount and regularity of watering depend on the plants, the soil's quality, and the growing conditions. If it's super hot or windy, chances are plants will need more water. If it's cool and cloudy, plants can generally go longer between waterings or go unwatered until temperatures rise.

The best way to understand how much water is enough is to check the soil by looking closely. Does it feel and look dry or damp, and at what depth? The soil surface may be bone dry, but an inch down, it may be just right.

Ollas have been used as watering devices for thousands of years. Once filled, these unglazed clay vessels release water as the soil dries, ensuring even watering as needed.

What's the best way to protect your garden from unwanted visitors?

It's incredibly disappointing to find the garden you've planted disappear, most likely eaten alive by animals like birds, deer, or ground squirrels. Equally as

SIGNS OF COMMON NUTRIENT DEFICIENCIES

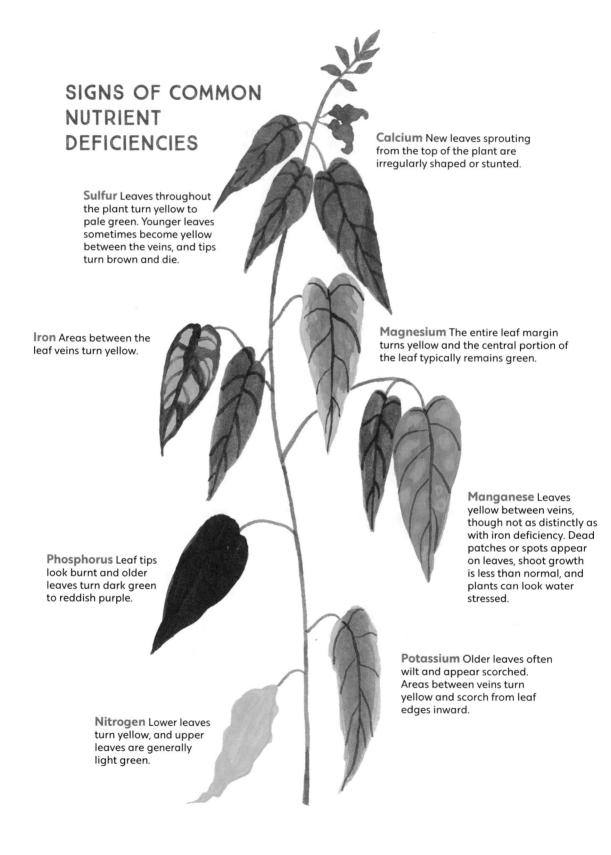

Calcium New leaves sprouting from the top of the plant are irregularly shaped or stunted.

Sulfur Leaves throughout the plant turn yellow to pale green. Younger leaves sometimes become yellow between the veins, and tips turn brown and die.

Iron Areas between the leaf veins turn yellow.

Magnesium The entire leaf margin turns yellow and the central portion of the leaf typically remains green.

Manganese Leaves yellow between veins, though not as distinctly as with iron deficiency. Dead patches or spots appear on leaves, shoot growth is less than normal, and plants can look water stressed.

Phosphorus Leaf tips look burnt and older leaves turn dark green to reddish purple.

Potassium Older leaves often wilt and appear scorched. Areas between veins turn yellow and scorch from leaf edges inward.

Nitrogen Lower leaves turn yellow, and upper leaves are generally light green.

Barriers and companion plants are often the best solutions for working with animals ready to eat your garden before you do.

frustrating is to discover the handiwork of tiny creatures like beetles and caterpillars. You may not ever lay eyes on them, but their telltale signs can't be missed.

However, before you devise a plan for who you'd like to keep out of your garden, consider who you'd like to invite in. Your garden is an ecosystem, after all, and as a gardener, you're a steward of your plot of earth. The leaves you find nibbled are, quite often, something to celebrate. Perhaps the larvae of swallowtail butterflies have made your garden their home, or maybe the semicircles missing from the margins of leaves are the handiwork of leafcutting bees. So, as with watering, the answer to the best way to protect your garden from unwanted visitors is, it depends. There's no one right solution but rather a myriad of solutions that ask us to think like an ecosystem. Tolerance is also a helpful tool. Our efforts to revive and regenerate our communities one plot at a time require each of us to rewire how we perceive pests and to reconsider beauty.

I found this chicken wire cloche in the demonstration garden at the Gardener's Supply headquarters in Burlington, Vermont. The cloche is quite effective. Notice the bare stems extending past it where leaves have been eaten?

That said, my tried-and-true suggestion is to plan how you'll manage unwanted visitors before you begin. Have you heard the saying, fences make good neighbors? The same is true for your garden. A well-constructed barrier, cloche, fabric, or wire system could be all you need to keep larger animals out. For insects, row covers and diatomaceous earth are excellent organic solutions to prevent them from eating everything in one go.

The next best thing after barriers is to grow a mix of plants. Grow companions, as described in the next chapter, including trap crops to lure pests away from prized plants. Smart plant pairings and healthy soil help protect your garden organically, with no need for toxic sprays and insecticides that harm the environment indiscriminately.

Slugs and snails often slide under the radar of the usual pest-mitigating barriers and require extra measures for successful management. If you're experiencing a slug invasion, first reduce their hiding spots. Work with compost instead of straw and consider making raised beds without overhanging caps. Or look to their potential cool and dark hiding spots to pick them off and remove them from the garden. Other measures I've found helpful include sprinkling coffee grounds, eggshells, or diatomaceous earth on the soil surface. You can also set up beer traps and welcome predators like birds and frogs.

Snails can slide under the radar to damage your plants. Look for them in cool and dark hiding spots.

NONFERTILIZER FERTILIZING

Regardless of the type of soil a plant prefers, most food crops need feeding (because they're feeding you and me, after all) and with materials derived from similar plants. Plan to give them compost infused with food scraps and mineral-rich activators. With woody plants such as trees and shrubs, feed them with materials similar to their particular makeup, such as wood chips and other high-carbon materials like leaves or dried grass trimmings.

It's usually only container plantings that need true fertilizing, because they're confined to a small space with an equally small soil ecosystem. This means both the soil and the plants are entirely reliant upon you for necessary inputs of nutrients. Because soil in containers tends to become dense and compacted, choosing (or making) the right fertilizer is key.

You can make your own nutrient-rich fertilizer and avoid synthetic fertilizers by brewing it. Yep. Brewing it. Make a tea out of compost, manure, or plants like comfrey and nettles.

With manure or compost, you can simply toss a few handfuls in a bucket, fill the bucket with water, and let it infuse like tea. After about twenty-four hours, strain off the liquid and apply it to your garden. You can also increase the microbial populations by aerating it as you make it. Simply insert an aerating pump like ones for fish tanks and let it bubble for twenty-four hours before you use the tea.

Damage caused by the production and use of **synthetic fertilizers, pesticides, and herbicides** goes beyond the immediate soil environment and the plants they're attempting to address. The process of making artificial fertilizers generates significant greenhouse gas emissions. When applied, these fertilizers pollute groundwater, drinking water, streams, and oceans through leaching and runoff.

Plants growing in the ground or large raised beds are best kept fed with a helping of compost and aged manures once or twice a year, depending on your climate. Simply top-dress them with 2 to 3 inches (5 to 7.5 centimeters) of compost or composted manure. To give crops a boost during the growing season, apply compost or other teas when plants look like they need it. Foliar feeding with comfrey and compost tea can also be beneficial and help ward off issues such as powdery mildew.

Soil pH is another factor to consider. Plants and soil microbes are adapted to particular soil pH ranges for optimal function and nutrient exchange, with many preferring a neutral soil pH. (The pH scale ranges from 0 to 14, with 6.5 to 7.5 considered neutral.) So, it's helpful to understand the pH of your soil before you begin planting to ensure the plants you're growing thrive. To test the pH of your soil, send it to a lab or use a store-bought testing device. If your soil is too acid or alkaline, you can amend it. Compost is a natural pH buffer and an excellent place to begin. You can make an acidic soil more alkaline by adding lime or make an alkaline soil more acidic by adding elemental sulfur. Amend sparingly and when in doubt, seek further advice from your university extension, soil testing laboratory, or soil association.

MAKE YOUR OWN COMFREY OR NETTLE TEA

A two-container, no-water system:

1. Densely pack a terra-cotta pot (with a drain hole) with torn leaves of comfrey or nettles. Then place the pot in a bucket (with no drain hole) and cover.

2. Let it sit for eight to twelve weeks out of direct sun. Eventually, a black sludgelike liquid will collect in the bucket.

3. Once the leaves have mostly decomposed, pour this tea off into a container.

4. Dilute it, 1 part tea to 20 parts water. This is about 2 cups (.5 liters) tea to 5 gallons (20 liters) of water.

5. Apply as needed.

Comfrey leaves for tea

To avoid being overwhelmed with tomatoes, plant them in batches three weeks to a month apart.

HARVESTING YOUR PRODUCE

Your plants are growing. Now what? Knowing when and how to harvest can feel a little unnerving if you're new to it. Even if you're a veteran gardener, it can be overwhelming—especially if everything you've grown is ready all at once.

So, let's back up for a moment. One of the best ways to harvest is little and often. Or, put another way, gather what you need when you need it. A handful of greens a day for salads and sandwiches, enough cucumbers and berries for snacking, or carrots for soups and slaws, and your garden is now a reservoir of groceries growing with ultimate freshness on demand.

To do this, you first need to sow little and often. This is commonly referred to as succession planting. It asks you to plant small batches of seeds or starts in intervals. The length of time between intervals depends on the length of the growing season for a particular plant. For crops with short growing seasons like radishes or lettuces, plant a new row each week if you have the space. Sow carrots from seed every couple of weeks, and for crops with longer growing seasons like cucumbers, green beans, and even particular tomatoes, plant a fresh batch about three weeks to a month after the first batch.

TOP LEFT: To harvest, pinch peas and beans off just above the pods. **TOP RIGHT:** Twist cucumbers and squash from the vine **ABOVE AND LEFT:** Several different varieties of cucumbers are growing on this single A-frame trellis. Of them, green apple (which Sinéad is holding), lemon, and Row 7 Seed Company's cucumber are our favorites.

Here are the basics of harvesting:

- Gather leaves from the outside in.
- Pluck beans and peas off the vine by pinching them off at the stem just above the fruit with your thumb and forefinger.
- Twist squash, cucumbers, and melons from the vine or use clippers to cut them free.
- Some tomatoes come free simply by lifting at an angle, and some require twisting. Either way, ripe tomatoes release freely and smell fragrant.
- Most berries require a gentle tug. If they don't release, they're not ready.

METHODS OF HOME PRESERVING

One of the indelible memories of my childhood is of my mom canning the pears from my grandfather's trees—peeling and quartering them, and filling jars one by one. We harvested them from a small orchard that produced far more fruit than any one family could consume, but this was the point—abundance is an insurance policy. The pears preserved in sugar to enjoy during the winter months tethered us to the seasons. The same is true of accidental bumper crops. They're an opportunity for home preserving and enjoying through the seasons. Experiment with a variety of methods.

Sun drying (fruits only) Hot, breezy, low-humidity days are best for sun drying. (This is not a suitable preserving method for high-humidity regions.) You need a constant temperature of 86 degrees F (30 degrees C) with a humidity of 60 percent or less to successfully sun dry fruits. Only sun dry high-sugar fruits, not vegetables or meats. Slice the fruit thin and place outside in full sun on food-grade wood or metals trays in a single layer. Bring inside or cover at night. Once drying is complete (one or two weeks), pasteurize by freezing for forty-eight hours or by placing in a preheated oven at 160 degrees F (71 degrees C) for thirty minutes.

Solar drying You can use the sun to power a greenhouse-like drying oven. Like with sun drying, stick to high-sugar fruits and pasteurize once the drying process is complete. Ventilation plus heat created with glass and a reflective foil surface decrease the drying time. The shorter drying times of solar drying reduce the risk of food spoilage. Search online for plans to build your own.

Oven drying and dehydrating You can also dehydrate fruits, vegetables, and meats in an oven or dedicated dehydrator at 140 degrees F (60 degrees C). Ovens are fine for occasional food drying but aren't as energy efficient as a food dehydrator, which is a small appliance with a heating element and fan that can be bought or made. Ovens without fans take nearly twice as long as a dehydrator. The length of time it takes to dehydrate foods varies with the type of food and its moisture content. Nutrients sensitive to heat such as vitamins C and A are compromised during the drying process, yet not all nutrition is lost, and dried foods are high in fiber.

Freezing Freezing produce is one of the most straightforward storage solutions. It maintains freshness and nutrition, especially if crops go directly from the garden to the freezer. Wash and dry produce before filling freezer-worthy containers. Try skipping plastic and use canning jars or airtight stainless steel food storage containers. If using jars, leave an inch of headspace at the top and keep the lid off until frozen. Once the food is frozen, add a layer of ice or water on top for further protection from air to prevent freezer burn. Wash off the ice before use.

Canning and pickling It's possible to quick pickle veggies and fruits by pouring a mixture of hot brine over them and storing them in the refrigerator. For longer shelf life, can and pickle crops in a hot water

bath. Be sure to sterilize containers before filling by either running them through your dishwasher or boiling them. Different foods have different requirements for safe and successful canning. Check with your national canning association (in the United States, the National Center for Home Food Preservation) or look for a trusted guide on home canning for the best results.

Fermentation Fermentation is the age-old process of using bacteria to preserve foods and transform flavor. The cool thing is that fermentation enhances the nutrient content of food while introducing more good bacteria to your body, ultimately making you healthier. Sterile jars, clean vegetables, and a clean work surface are musts for successful fermentation. Use salt, whey, or a starter culture and filtered water. Pack jars full and weigh the contents down with a plate or a fermenting weight to keep it

Pickled vegetables

under liquid and in an anaerobic state. Check on each jar daily, and when it smells sour, it's probably ready. If it stinks, throw it out and try again. If you're still uncertain about the fermenting process, consider throwing a fermenting party and include friends with more experience to learn tricks and recipes.

Root cellar and cold storage Many fruits and vegetables can last for weeks or months in cold storage. Root vegetables, brassicas, melons, squash, and leafy greens are all good candidates, with varying storage lives. You can use an existing basement or dig a root cellar. A dark space with ventilation and humidity of 80 to 95 percent to keep produce from drying out is essential. An earth or gravel floor helps maintain a cool, humid environment, and the naturally antibacterial nature of wood makes it the perfect material for shelving and bins.

TOP LEFT: Tomatoes (which are actually fruits) ready for sun or solar drying **TOP RIGHT**: Dehydrated persimmons **ABOVE**: Fermented cabbage **LEFT**: Frozen strawberries

REWILDING TO SUPPORT BIODIVERSITY

DID YOU KNOW THAT HONEYBEE COLONIES ARE DEFINED IN PART BY THE MICROBES THAT INHABIT INDIVIDUAL BEES? Guard bees tasked with defending their hive from potential marauding bees identify imposters by their unique odor. It turns out bee odor is produced by cohabiting microbes—very much like with us. (It's true, we have bacteria to thank for our bodily bouquet.) And, like us, they acquire their microbiome from food, nature, and each other. Like us, too, the bacteria that bees coexist with increase their resiliency, protecting them from harmful viruses and disease.

Everything in the universe is hitched to everything else.

Our highly complex world reminds us that no one thing can be removed without impacting all other things. John Muir is known for coining this idea when he said: "When we try to pick out anything by itself, we find it hitched to everything else in the Universe." Remove microbes, and what happens to bees? Is a bee still a bee without its microbial partners? What happens to us and the earth beneath our feet without these microscopic friends?

With approximately 50 percent of the human genome composed of bacteria, it's clear that part of being human is being part microbe. Science tells us we couldn't survive without this symbiosis, and we thrive the more biodiverse the microbiome, which reflects the biodiversity of the greater biome, our home planet: from soil to insects to flowers to trees. You could say that we're hitched not just to microbes but to all living things, and the same assumption can be made for creatures like bees.

Like my garden, your outdoor space—and the surrounding community—is already home to countless creatures, most of which you've likely never seen, but they're there in between the leaves and soil and branches. What's better still is that our homes and cityscapes can quickly become gardensteads, places tended with thoughtful planning and planting to support an ever-greater abundance of biodiversity while enlivening resilient ecosystems and communities.

THE ROLE OF NATIVE PLANTS

Native plants are plants specific to a region or ecological niche that have coadapted with the endemic insects, birds, and other wildlife throughout natural history, many over hundreds of thousands of years and longer. Consider, for a moment, that some individual plants such as bristlecone pines are roughly five thousand years old. Think of their evolutionary time frame and the ecosystem that's come to rely on them, as they have come to rely on it. Plants are coevolutionary partners, adapting hand in hand with soil, soil microbes, and the other creatures living in soil, as well as neighboring plants, insects, birds, and the countless other animals living aboveground.

The shapes and behaviors of both plants and animals reflect the collaborative dance they've been performing for eons. Blooms with landing pads such as those of Joe Pye weed, zinnias, and Mexican sunflowers give pollinators like butterflies a platform to stop and forage. Alternately, the size of a bee's tongue determines which flowers it can visit. Some bees are generalists and can visit almost any flower, while others are closely matched with the flowers they've evolved with over centuries. Bees with long tongues like bumblebees require inflorescences with equally long flower parts.

LEFT: Somewhere along the evolutionary timeline, pollinators like bees and flowering plants like this African blue basil formed symbiotic relationships in which they mutually benefit. **RIGHT:** I came across this rattlesnake master, *Eryngium yuccifolium*, in the Gardener's Supply demonstration garden in Burlington, Vermont. While not a true native of New England, it's native to the south and central areas of the United States, and this particular plant had the greatest number and diversity of insect visitors of any plant in the garden that day.

PLANT WITH PURPOSE

When you're approaching your plot, ask yourself, What would nature do? If you were to create a nature-based landscape that rewilds your portion of this big, beautiful planet, how would it look and what sounds would you hear? What plants would you find?

This is what artist and garden designer Pam Karlson set out to do. When she and her husband bought their Chicago home in 1991, she dreamed of giving her yard back to nature while finding a way to pay homage to the Native Americans who had lived there long before her. She wasn't daunted by the fact that the Kennedy Expressway is a half block away or that the approach for O'Hare International Airport is directly overhead. Their collective din wasn't a hindrance but an inspiration. She saw her 50-by-100-foot (15-by-30-meter) backyard as the refuge it's become—a resting place for migratory birds and home to countless butterflies and bees.

Pam discovered that as she added trees and water features and slowly swapped out nonnative plants for natives, the bird count in her backyard rose at a similar rate. She's cataloged more than a hundred different bird species in her plot alone. The neighboring lots dedicated to lawn and pavement appeared empty in comparison during my visit.

Something else happened too. When Pam gave her yard to nature, she in turn gave nature to herself. For Pam, her garden is an example of hope that is as much her passion as it is a place of healing.

In California, designer Robert Hewitt of Girasole Sonoma supports biodiversity with whimsical plant pairings. His front yard pollinator garden is composed of native, ornamental, and edible plants. By incorporating the hellstrip (the area between the sidewalk and the street), he expands his real estate, making it a favorite route for neighbors to walk and a welcome plot of habitat for birds and pollinators.

Planting with the purpose of supporting biodiversity, as Pam and Robert have done, is an intention-driven process inspired by a vision of a specific outcome. It's also a process that asks you to embrace a willingness to learn and grow as your garden grows.

TOP: Pam transformed her back yard into an oasis for migratory birds with the help of native plants, her "bird tree" (a hawthorn), and water features. **CENTER:** Pam does her best to add native plants, such as red cardinal flower (*Lobelia cardinalis*), to her garden. Native plants have coadapted with endemic wildlife and are best suited for supporting and fostering biodiversity.
RIGHT: This American goldfinch is at home in Pam's Chicago garden.

Among the many plants you'll find in Robert Hewitt's front yard garden are *Verbena bonariensis*, fennel, bunchgrasses, agastache, and a handful of cardoons. While not native to California, each of these plants is a beneficial wildlife plant. California buckwheat, also present, with clusters of tiny white flowers held aloft, is a native, as are the milkweeds sprinkled throughout.

HOW TO PLANT TO SUPPORT BIODIVERSITY

- Begin one plant at a time.

- Use what you learned when assessing your site. What's your climate, topography, and available light?

- Assess your goals. Would you like to plant a garden for wildlife, flowers for cutting, perennials for sequestering carbon, and kitchen garden edibles? Perhaps, like Pam, you'd like to consider the natural and cultural history of the landscape?

- Next, create a running list of plants native to your region that complement your aesthetic and use this list as a starting point.

- Swap out low-functioning ornamentals for natives. This doesn't mean you have to give up your favorite hollyhocks or daylilies, but find a happy medium between natives and nonnative plantings. Striving for 50 percent native plantings is a good initial goal.

Aim to grow natives as half of your ornamental landscape plants.

BIODIVERSITY BEGETS BIODIVERSITY

While there's still much to learn about the ecological relationships of plants, animals, and other organisms living above and below the ground, it's clear that feedback loops connect them all. They interact in a complex give-and-take that's formed throughout Earth's natural history. These interactions can also be considered stressors where organisms push and pull each other along in their life cycles. For instance, the larvae of swallowtail butterflies consume the leaves of their host plants, which are in the carrot or parsley family (scientifically known as Apiaceae). As adult butterflies, swallowtails pollinate the same plants they were chewing on weeks before. Together, each of these sets of species ensures the survival of the other.

It's also true that the push-and-pull of life within ecological communities affects species even when it's not immediately apparent. If you remember, it's the bacteria within bees that help them distinguish a friend from a foe. Each bee is home to all sorts of bacteria. These bacteria are essential vectors, couriering bacteria from plants and soil to each other, and so on. Relationships and forces like these support biodiversity as a whole.

If we consider these relationships from the ground up, feedback loops between soil organisms and plants contribute to plant and soil diversity. Meanwhile, feedback loops between plants, insects (such as swallowtail butterflies and bees), and wildlife contribute to plant and wildlife diversity. It's the connection between plant-and-wildlife and soil-and-plant feedback loops that creates the push and pull that leads to the stability—and survival—of each of these groups. The more robust and biodiverse a system, the more resilient it is.

Ecologically speaking, it's biodiversity itself that encourages the continued diversifying of life. As species form in the evolutionary process, they create an ever-greater number of niches for other species to fill, spurring along the process of coevolving species richness.

It's also been found time and again that the more biodiversity a landscape hosts, the more resilient the landscape becomes, particularly in the face of global concerns such as drought and other extreme weather events. Conversely, when we lose species as we are now, the riot of life that rubs shoulders, vying for resources, is at risk—ultimately leading to the breakdown of ecosystems.

Feedback loops between plants and insects contribute to both plant and insect diversity.

Feedback loops between plants and soil organisms contribute to plant and soil diversity.

Biodiversity feedback loops at work. Life aboveground impacts life belowground. Equally, soil life directly impacts the health and biodiversity of plants and life aboveground.

Cardoons like this one are favorites of both birds and insect pollinators.

WHEN INSECTS DISAPPEAR

American biologist and naturalist E.O. Wilson has said, "If all mankind were to disappear, the world would regenerate back to the rich state of equilibrium that existed ten thousand years ago. If insects were to vanish, the environment would collapse into chaos." We've reached a juncture, a precipitous tipping point. What do we do about the loss of the world's insects—its bees, hoverflies, butterflies, and the many other creatures we don't give much attention to except when finding them in places we'd rather not?

A 2019 review published in the journal *Biological Conservation* found that one-third of the world's insects are at risk. With the current rate of decline averaging about 2.5 percent a year, we'll lose all of the world's insects within the next century. With more than three-quarters of global food crops reliant on pollinating

Milkweed beetles rely on milkweed as their host plant, much like monarchs. Interestingly, they produce the same vibrant color scheme as monarchs to warn potential predators to stay away. "Don't eat me, I'm toxic!"

insects, the ramifications of their decline is ominous—not just for us, but also for our planet.

One of the many groups of insects struggling to survive is bees. They're on the brink of extinction. The rare bee specialists are at the greatest risk. As the earth warms and habitats shrink in size, the opportunity for their survival declines at an equally alarming rate. If we take a close look at bumblebees alone, we find that the increasing number of unusually hot days is increasing regionalized extinction. In North America, their population has declined by 50 percent in less than fifty years, meaning we're now 50 percent less likely to see a bumblebee than we were before 1974.

Organizations such as the Xerces Society are working to overturn a court ruling in California that **excludes insects** from the protections of the California Endangered Species Act.

Yet, it doesn't have to be this way. We can shift the balance in favor of a healthy, life-filled planet. Where do we begin? We can Grow Now.

GROWING HABITAT STARTS AT HOME

Habitat fragmentation occurs when large expanses of land are broken into smaller, isolated parcels. Trees are cut, houses are built, cities expand, and industry and conventional farms replace wilderness. The thing is, habitats rely on connectivity. When we carve up landscapes, we disenfranchise whole groups of plants and animals, cutting them off from the wonderfully complex systems upon which they rely. The climate crisis adds insult to injury, fueling the problem while shrinking habitable landscapes.

We can grow habitat and offset habitat fragmentation by planting with the purpose of supporting biodiversity in our home plots and cityscapes. When we take the bird's-eye view, we can look for thoughtful ways to connect these spaces into living greenways.

You've got this! You can connect and **rewild** our planet starting with your home plot, community garden, schoolyard, rooftop, and the unused spaces along city blocks. And together, your efforts and my efforts and the efforts of our neighbors work collectively. We can support the complex natural matrix of

ABOVE: Populations of pollinating insects have fallen quickly in the last few decades, with ominous ramifications. But we can shift the balance in their favor when we regenerate landscapes and connect living greenways. **RIGHT:** Garden companions such as Mexican sunflowers (*Tithonia rotundifolia*) and African blue basil are pollinator all-stars. Monarch butterflies are particularly fond of Mexican sunflowers.

microbe-rich systems we each rely on for our health, the health of our families, and the health of our planet.

The equation we're after is my garden + your garden + your neighbor's garden = save the planet one garden at a time. However, we can go one step farther and, if you remember the order of operations from Algebra 1, the equation is more like this: (my garden + your garden + your neighbor's garden) (community green spaces + parks + greenways + wild places + beyond-organic farms) = save the planet one garden at a time.

Thoughtfully planted gardens are veritable lifelines for rewilding our home planet, reminding us that what is local is global.

A three-year survey conducted by the University of Bristol found that our urban and suburban landscapes are potential havens for biodiversity. Farm fields may be feast or famine for wildlife, but villages, towns, and cityscapes are filled with habitat—an abundant and diverse range of plants and flowers blooming through the seasons. Even our kitchen garden plots play a vital role. Here lies the power to save pollinators, insects, and ourselves.

It's easy to see the possible benefits of our collective efforts and gardens with this aerial perspective. Designer Robert Hewitt's front yard garden is at center with the curving path.

The study made these key suggestions:

- Grow a garden and increase the number and size of community gardens.
- Mow less, shrink your lawn, and if you do have a lawn, mix turf with flowering plants.
- Encourage a diversity of plantings that bloom through the seasons.
- Grow fruits, vegetables, and companions.
- Focus on plants preferred by pollinators such as natives and select ornamentals.
- Give certain weeds like dandelions room to grow.

GARDEN PLANTS MOST VISITED DURING THE STUDY

blackberries
borage
buttercups
comfrey
dandelions
lavender
marigolds
thistles

Nature is the best at rewilding. We're merely doing what we can to keep up, help out, and mimic her ways, using techniques such as companion planting, interplanting, growing a food forest, creating edges and ecotones, and building

Bluma Flower Farm in Berkeley, CA, is not only a farm but also a biodiversity reservoir.

ABOVE: Look closely and you can see the hummingbird visiting Bluma Flower Farm.
RIGHT: Evergreen shrubs like this bush chinquapin growing on the rooftop at Bluma Flower Farm maintain living roots in the ground and support biodiversity.

TOP LEFT: A black phoebe rests in a native perennial wildflower meadow. **TOP RIGHT:** A honeybee visits a lavender plant. **ABOVE:** A California quail finds a perch in Sonoma Garden Park.

This was the summer when I decided to throw all caution to the wind and grow a garden jungle. It was wonderful. I had zero issues with pests, and loads of pollinators. The only trouble was moving about and reaching the center of the garden to harvest.

homes for wildlife. These are nature-based solutions; simultaneously, they're a language—dialogue through action, if you will—for growing healthier humans and healthier habitats.

COMPANION PLANTING

In its simplest terms, companion planting is the thoughtful pairing of different plants to protect them from pests and help them grow. While it's generally a term applied to food gardens, it's a useful, commonsense concept for understanding the complex relationships of plants, not just to each other but also to the big, wide world in which they grow.

Why not add chives, calendula, and herbs like thyme to your garden? The mashup of pungent and uniquely aromatic fragrances confuses pests like carrot flies that rely on their sense of smell to find their way. (Carrot flies can smell

Rudbeckias are pollinator-friendly companion plants.

TOP: Plants in the mustard family like these starts are known to contain compounds that reduce soil pathogens. Some organic strawberry growers utilize mustards between strawberry plantings or in crop rotations to reduce strawberry diseases. **ABOVE:** Borage is interplanted with tomatoes to attract beneficial insects.

I always grow basil and marigolds near my tomatoes.

Nasturtiums are a reliable companion to brassicas such as kale and broccoli.

unearthed and newly thinned carrots from miles away!) There are other combinations too. For instance, I always grow basil and marigolds near my tomatoes. It's consistently been a winning plant pairing, and growing tomatoes and basil side by side means it's easy to harvest them together for the many recipes calling for both.

Nasturtiums can act as a **trap crop**, luring pests like aphids away from brassicas such as kale and broccoli. Just note that for trap crops to be truly effective, it's important to place them 15 feet (4.5 meters) away from the crop you'd like to protect.

The soil is emboldened with companion planting too. If you remember, different plants collaborate with different soil organisms. So diversifying plant groups inherently diversifies the biology living within the soil, creating a more resilient system as a whole.

Let's also not forget the role of pollinator-friendly companions. You'll have no trouble attracting the beneficial insects and birds needed for a thriving and productive garden with plants like borage, zinnias, ornamental basil, chamomile, and thyme.

INTERPLANTING

How might your plants best coexist, support biodiversity, and make the most of the square yards (or feet) you have on hand? Interplanting explores these questions with numerous points of entry.

Begin with a commonsense approach and work with plants' growth habits and maturation times to increase productivity and optimize space. To do this, grow taller plants such as sunflowers at the north end of beds, sun-loving crops to their south, and plants that require afternoon shade such as leafy greens and parsley to the north of both. It's also possible to grow successions of quick-growing crops like radishes, lettuces, and cilantro among plants with multimonth growing seasons such as Tuscan kale, chard, and tomatoes.

A three sisters planting combines corn, squash, and beans. The corn stalks support the twining beans, and the squash keeps the ground covered. The combination is an excellent starting point for gardening with children.

Another interplanting duo I rely on is the pairing of radishes and carrots. Sow them side by side. The radishes will be up and out long before the carrots are ready, and the quick-emerging radish sprouts will remind you where you planted your carrots (something I sometimes have trouble remembering, especially because carrots always seem to take an excruciatingly long time to germinate).

Native Americans historically interplanted a set of crops they called the three sisters. Have you heard of them? It's the combination of corn, beans, and squash, and the numerous legends of the three sisters revolve around their bond and relationship to one another. To grow a three sisters garden, simply sow beans around corn and plant squash at their feet. The corn is sturdy and rises tall, providing the support that pole beans need. Beans are soil builders, fixing nitrogen in the ground thanks to their relationship with rhizobia bacteria, which is helpful because corn tends to be a heavy feeder. And squash covers ground, helping prevent weed growth, retain soil moisture, and moderate soil temperatures. You'll sometimes see sunflowers in the place of corn, and historically, some Native American peoples are also known to have added Rocky Mountain bee plant (*Cleome serrulata*) to the mix to encourage pollination.

Use interplanting techniques in flower gardens, perennial borders, and larger landscapes to achieve many of the same goals as in food gardens: cover ground, optimize space, and let the plants do much of the work of caring for soil while creating habitat for wildlife.

EDGES AND ECOTONES

It turns out that the edges of ecosystems are biodiversity-rich hubs. Have you ever stepped out of a forest into a meadow to find an unbelievable number of birds and insects darting about, skipping from grass to flower? Or perhaps you've noticed the shift in animal and plant life when approaching a stream or lake? The complex intersection of conditions at the edges of ecological niches is ripe for life.

In nature, the transition from one biological community to another is an *ecotone*—a word born from the two words *ecology* and *-tone*, derived from the Greek *tonos*, meaning tension. Ecotones form when distinct communities blend gradually or abruptly. An edge is exactly what you might expect, the place or line

Kelsey Adams of West Lane Flowers in Burlington, Vermont, mixes vegetables and herbs with some of her cutting garden plants to cover ground, work together as companions, and optimize space.

GROW A FOOD FOREST

Forests exist without help from us. Trees, shrubs, and understory plants find their place within complex systems. Nutrients, including carbon, are recycled, and carbon is naturally sequestered. They're inherently no-dig organic systems filled with biodiversity. If we were to hit the rewind button on making a mature forest system, we'd see the play-by-play of how it formed. If you can imagine what this might look like, use this as a roadmap to grow a forest garden of your own.

I was lucky enough to visit Eric Toensmeier's personal forest garden one summer while visiting New England. It's a narrow row house lot packed from corner to corner with a riot of perennial currants, gooseberries, greens like sea kale, hardy kiwis, fruit trees, and ferns interwoven with nitrogen-fixing ground covers and annuals.

Eric is the author of *Paradise Lot*, *Perennial Vegetables*, and *The Carbon Farming Solution*, and coauthor of *Edible Forest Gardens*. He's also a lecturer at Yale University and a senior biosequestration fellow with Project Drawdown. As he's measured it, his 4,360-square-foot (405-square-meter) edible forest garden, pictured here, sequesters enough carbon every ten years to offset the average American adult's annual carbon footprint! As you can see, it's composed of layers of edible perennials designed to mimic ecosystems found in nature. Here, Eric and his family harvest a host of edibles eleven months out of the year, even during the coldest winter months, thanks to regenerative soil practices and careful plant selection.

To create your own food forest, consider growing an overstory layer of trees with varied understory plants tucked beneath them, including smaller trees and shrubs, perennials, self-seeding annuals, vines, and ground covers.

ERIC'S TOP TEN NUTRITIOUS PERENNIAL PLANT PICKS

blueberries and huckleberries (*Vaccinium* species)

Chinese toon (*Toona sinensis*)

edible-leaf mulberry (*Morus alba* and hybrids)

gooseberries and currants, including native species (*Ribes* species)

grape (*Vitis vinifera* and related species)

grape leaves (*Vitis vinifera* and related species)

juneberries and saskatoons (*Amelanchier* species)

milkweed (*Asclepias syriaca* and *A. speciosa*)

rose hips (*Rosa rugosa* and native species)

stinging nettle (*Urtica dioica* and related species)

NINE LAYERS OF A FOREST GARDEN

1. overstory canopy of trees
2. understory of smaller and younger trees
3. shrubs
4. herbaceous and evergreen perennials
5. root vegetables
6. ground covers
7. vines and vertical climbers
8. aquatic and wetland plants
9. fungi living in the soil and on other plants

One of the easiest ways to invite wildlife into your garden is to add a water feature.

where two different systems come together. What happens at the edges of systems is sometimes referred to as the edge effect.

You can easily create edges and ecotones in your garden and the landscapes closest to home. Add a water feature or mow a path through a meadow. Or add a perennial border around your food or flower garden, particularly one filled with native plants, and you're on your way to a biodiversity-rich ecotone grown at home.

HOMES FOR WILDLIFE

It was in one of my first gardens that I startled a toad from its home. We both jumped when I moved a rock aside—her from her hiding spot and me to my feet. I clearly remember the awe that washed over me, followed by an immediate sense of regret. How did I miss the signs that the hollowed-out opening under the rock was

An insect hotel in Sonoma Garden Park, a project of Sonoma Ecology Center, provides places for insects like solitary bees and wasps to shelter and nest.

the entry to a toad home? Yet, honestly, a toad was the last creature I expected to find living in that high mountain desert garden. It was only after she disappeared that I connected the dots and saw her residence for what it was: shady, cool, protected, and damp, with plenty of insects to eat—the perfect toad home.

Not that long ago, I discovered tiny native bees living in the hollowed-out stems of last year's raspberry canes. Just like the time I unknowingly routed the toad from its home, this was a moment when I was forced to pause and wonder, Who else lives here? And who else can I invite?

To figure this out, quietly observe your plot and survey who might be coming and going. Next, it helps to step inside the world of nature for perspective. If you were a bee, where would you live? What is your perfect home? It's also helpful to learn more about the animals native to your region so you can begin with intention. The homes you create are a direct function of who might inhabit them.

boxes
for birds

hotels for bugs

water for wildlife

homes for toads

bare ground for bees

dead seed heads for
birds and insects

EASY WAYS TO CREATE HOMES FOR WILDLIFE

- Make houses for bats, birds, and squirrels.

- Build an insect hotel with stems, branches, bark, and straw.

- Dig a pond or create other water features.

- Burrow a toad home in a shady spot not too far from water and food, and cover part of its entrance with a stone or branch.

- Create bird feeders in the cover of leaves and high branches to protect them from house cats.

- Leave some patches of earth uncovered and mulch free for ground nesting bees.

- Wait to clean up your fall garden until spring and even then, do so sparingly. Fallen leaves and dead branches, stems, and flowers are habitats for various insects and other animals.

- Mow your lawn less or convert it into a wildflower meadow or an expanded garden.

- Leave room for wildlife corridors. Who might need to pass through your area, and how will they get there?

- Make your own compost. Compost piles are havens for wildlife like worms and salamanders, and other, larger animals like racoons, opposums, and rats if not enclosed in wire or another protective barrier.

LIVING GREENWAYS

What we often miss when looking out over a landscape are creatures like ants moving bits of leaves from tree to home, mice making it their business to forage endlessly, or owls hunting for those same mice. Neither do we see the groundwater running beneath the roots of trees or that same system of roots paired with fungi and soil protecting communities from floods while doing the work of cycling and sequestering carbon.

Living greenways are the corridors, paths, and points of connection where nature-filled places meet. They provide opportunities for ecological islands, fragmented through human activity, to come together and coexist, creating larger areas of ecological significance. They can take various shapes. Parks, nature reserves, protected river systems, regenerative farms, and gardens are a few. They allow nature and the many animals found in nature, such as ants and owls, to move freely, and landscapes to function as a whole—to thrive. When connected, nature-filled places ultimately provide far more benefits than when separated.

Like gardens, living greenways aren't just for wildlife; they're also essential for people. Did you know that children have improved concentration after a walk through a park? Time in nature nourishes our ability to learn. Equally, the presence and volume of trail systems, parks, riverwalks, reclaimed vacant lots, gardens, and open spaces increase everything from property values to your personal happiness quotient.

Remember the biodiversity hypothesis? Increasing connectivity to nature directly impacts your physical and emotional well-being, addressing everything from allergies to anxiety. Parks and green spaces also provide places to gather, exercise, and relax. These same green spaces help keep the carbon cycle moving in a net positive direction and double as a natural filter, helping control floods while safeguarding waterways, keeping them clean. When we plant our gardens and city-scapes with intention, collaborate with one another, care for soil, set aside areas to rewild, and leave wild places wild, we actively create living greenways.

Nature is made up of worlds within worlds, and even the smallest patches and plots of undisturbed habitats and garden systems are brimming with biodiversity. Ecology reminds us that these same systems are far more effective at supporting wild things (and people) the greater the connectivity. Fill in the gaps with leafy, verdant life, and now we're onto something resilient and wonderful—a system that has the ability to temper the climate crisis, mitigate species extinction, and green a path to healthier families and communities.

Just think of the possibilities! Living greenways form with thoughtful planning and planting. When we use no-dig, regenerative organic principles to foster biodiversity and sequester carbon in soil, we grow healthy communities and a resilient planet.

GROW
MORE
GOOD

AN IDEA KNOWN AS THE BUTTERFLY EFFECT reminds us of the hidden connections among all things, suggesting that the flapping of a butterfly's wings has the potential to influence the path of a typhoon halfway around the world. While this analogy may be an exaggeration, there's something to it. Tiny acts have big impacts, in your personal life and in the world.

In their book *Good Omens*, Terry Pratchett and Neil Gaiman write: "It used to be thought that events that changed the world were things like big bombs, maniac politicians, huge earthquakes, and vast population movements, but it has now been realized that this is a very old-fashioned view. . . . The things that change the world, according to Chaos theory, are tiny things." Chaos theory, an interdisciplinary theory with mathematical roots, states that complex systems that appear to be random, in truth share underlying, interconnected patterns driven by self-organized feedback loops.

A California native sage lines a sidewalk, providing an oasis for beneficial insects.

Many factors determine how much carbon you can sequester in soil, but the benefits of beginning today are immediate.

When you look to the principles outlined in this book of going beyond organic, caring for soil, fostering biodiversity, growing hyperlocal food, and embracing nature, you'll discover you're growing more than a garden. You're growing a lifeline and a new way of seeing the world. With this seeing, this lens, comes a language we can share—and herein lies the power to shift the larger narrative around how we grow food, how we harness energy, and how we approach nature.

Begin planting today, share what you can't use, become a citizen scientist. Practice growing the change that you want to see and that you want to be.

WHAT YOU PLANT FOR TOMORROW, YOU GROW TODAY

The successful return of carbon to soil in our landscapes depends upon a complex matrix of variables. It's one of those oh-so-precise "it depends" models. You know

TWELVE TINY ACTS
TO IMPROVE YOUR LIFE

1   Smile more. Drink water. Carve out time for you.

2   Take five minutes a day to get your hands dirty, sow seeds, harvest what you grow, and make your own compost.

3   Grow what you love, such as your favorite herbs, greens, or flowers. Research reminds us that simply looking at plants decreases stress and elevates mood.

4   Plant nutrition. Eat with the seasons. Live hyperlocally—just think of the nutritional benefits and reduced carbon footprint that come with growing some of your own food.

5   Hug your family and feed them healthy food from the garden. Studies show that kids eat more fruits and vegetables when they're homegrown, and this goes for adults too.

6   Increase your nature quotient. Spend 20 minutes a day or 120 minutes a week in nature. Studies show that people who spend a minimum of 120 minutes per week in nature have decreased heart rates, lower blood pressure, less stress, improved concentration, and a greater overall sense of well-being.

7   Stay curious. If you're asking yourself, I wonder why . . . ? take time to explore and observe whatever may have caught your attention and learn more. You never know what you may discover.

8   Practice random acts of kindness.

9   Be generous. Grow native wildflowers in abandoned lots or along overlooked roadside verges.

10 Volunteer. I know you're busy. The bills need to get paid, you have dinner to cook, and the dog needs walking, but volunteering isn't just good for others; it's good for you. Much like time in nature, volunteering is known to decrease depression, keeping you active and curious.

11 Help in your community garden or school garden, or with organized plantings sponsored by your regional native plant society or wildlife trust.

12 Share what you grow.

ABOVE: Even often-forgotten patches of earth are vital to rewilding. RIGHT: Pollinator-friendly plants flourish near the entrance to the City Market Onion River Co-op in Burlington, Vermont.

the ones? Like earlier in this book when I shared ideas on when and how much to water your garden, in the end it comes down to "it depends." Quality of soil, air temperature, sun, wind, and what you're growing keep you on your toes and ask you to adapt—and live with "it depends."

The "it depends" model for soil carbon sequestration, particularly long-term carbon storage in soil, depends on variables such as how much compost and other organic matter you give your soil, how much digging you do, how arid or temperate your climate is, what your soil type is, and what you're growing. These all factor into how much carbon you can actively sequester in soil and how long it stays tucked away.

Because of these compounding variables, findings from research into how long it takes to store carbon in soil are all over the map. We do know through continued investigations that the process of restoring carbon to the soil takes decades. As much as we want it to happen overnight, it doesn't. It takes time. As frustrating as this may sound (because who doesn't wish for a magic wand to solve life's big problems?), it doesn't mean you shouldn't start the process of restoring soil and bringing life back to the places closest to home. Rather, start today. Don't wait. The benefits of beginning today are immediate.

POWER TO THE PEOPLE WHO PLANT

A growing number of organizations worldwide are actively working to green their communities while creating hyperlocal food hubs. Nicole Landers, who cofounded Community Healing Gardens and more recently cofounded the Los Angeles Children's Garden, has created a quiver of urban garden initiatives that lead by example.

Nicole was the genius behind feeding underserved neighborhoods of Los Angeles with curbside veggie boxes from which anyone could pick while offering on-the-job training in dedicated gardens and cooperative programs. For example, the Los Angeles Children's Garden is a community-based urban food and flower farm. It provides hands-on opportunities for families to participate in the farm, where they learn composting techniques and best practices for water and energy

Danielle Marquez (left) and Nicole Landers (right) harvest vegetables grown in an urban garden working to transform neighborhoods one garden at a time.

conservation. Biodiversity and observations of butterflies, bees, and birds are also central to their garden-based education.

It's possible to create your own initiative or organization based on the resources at hand and your community's needs. Several years ago, I started a neighborhood gleaning program where we pick unwanted fruit from trees. Some of the fruit (mainly apples and pears) is then pressed into cider to celebrate the abundance of food already growing in our yards and cities. The remaining portion is given to people in need by way of a nearby pantry and free farmer's market in San Francisco.

My hope is to not only share our abundance but to change the way we see these often-overlooked trees, reminding others of their inherent value and beauty. Since I began the program, I have repeatedly heard people say, "I started seeing apple trees everywhere!" Following this remark (though usually an exclamation), the conversation turns to the many other fruit trees left unpicked: trees such as loquats, citrus, persimmons, plums, pineapple guavas, and pomegranates.

Please
feel free to
eat me

COMMUNITY HEALING GARDENS

@eatbythe
bluesea

Curbside veggie boxes line the streets of Venice, California, a neighborhood of Los Angeles—anyone is free to harvest.

TOP LEFT: I don't know what I'd do without Sinéad's help. **TOP RIGHT:** Our friend Ward Flad donates apples from his trees every fall. He keeps them pruned so they're easily handpicked without a ladder or pole picker. **ABOVE:** Apples gleaned from community trees are pressed at our local harvest festival. **LEFT:** Extra fruit gets delivered to the free farmer's market in San Francisco.

SWAP. BARTER. GIVE.

When I was a little girl, my mom would send me on errands to fetch this or that from a friend down the lane or trust me to take eggs to Mrs. Molander, our neighbor, to complete her batch of cookies. Sometimes I'd return home with clippings of plants that my mom would root in a glass of water on the kitchen windowsill. (I loved watching their roots emerge and slowly fill the jar.) Other times I'd return with a cup of sugar or seeds for planting in our spring garden.

What goes around, comes around.

Believe it or not, I was a shy child, and when I began moonlighting as my mom's courier (perhaps as early as age five or six), being the sole and trusted guardian of those eggs, cuttings, and seeds during their trip from one home to the other was formative in giving me a sense of purpose and confidence. It was wonderfully important. The deep sense of community and belonging fostered by our neighborhood sharing economy is eternally hardwired within me. It moves me forward to this day (perhaps even sending me down the path to write this book).

The surplus fruit from your apple tree, the bumper crop of cucumbers you're tired of pickling, or the nasturtium seeds filling your planters may be exactly what a neighbor needs. Or it could be they're the perfect gift when passed along to friends and family. It also works the other way around: perhaps your neighbor's extra nasturtiums seeds are exactly what you were hoping to plant. A sharing economy is like a cross street with multiple intersections and works best when we each participate, giving and receiving what and when we can.

Become a citizen scientist with the help of your camera.

BECOME A CITIZEN SCIENTIST

There is power in numbers. The Cornell Lab of Ornithology's annual bird count, Global Big Day, tallied record-breaking numbers of birds in 2020. More biodiversity was recorded on this single day than at any other time in history. This was due in part to the sheer number of bird-watchers who took to the outdoors with their binoculars and cameras in the midst of the coronavirus pandemic. If a small group of scientists had tried to complete the same number of observations, it would have taken them years!

In North America, the Xerces Society leads an annual Thanksgiving count of western monarchs and hosts several other community science opportunities such as mapping milkweed and bumblebee encounters. The National Park Service in the United States has its own laundry list of opportunities, including such projects as sampling dragonfly larvae and mapping rare plants. In the United Kingdom, the

Wildlife Trusts empower regular people to survey seashores, rivers, and hedgerows. There are similar programs in nearly every corner of the globe, and each of them shines a light on the complex world in which we live, giving us an ever-greater chance to make sound decisions to move forward toward a better future.

WE ALL LOVE A GOOD STORY

The conversations that arise from the simple act of growing are as important as the acts themselves. Actions that become conversations become the narratives that shape worldviews. Equally as important are the words themselves. Rewriting the stories that no longer serve our communities and the planet require us to embrace language that supports the process. Or, it can work the other way around. Change your language, and you're on your way to changing your perceptions and behaviors—often accompanied by a net positive trickle-down effect.

Dr. Claudia Gross reminds us that words create worlds (if you remember, this is also the title of her book). Consider the word *sustain*. At an elementary level, it means to support. While it implies the act of providing sustenance, it also implies maintaining the status quo. Now compare it to *regenerate*. At an elementary level, it means to regrow. It's a word that immediately brings to mind a host of other words. Words like *restore, rewild, revive, and repair*.

LEFT: Citizen scientists can help conservation efforts by tallying birds or butterflies or any number of other subjects in the outdoors. **RIGHT:** Scabiosas and sunflowers grow in the Safe Place for Youth (SPY) garden in Venice, California.

WHERE TO LOOK TO CONTINUE GROWING

- First, search your community for a composting council or an organization like LA Compost. They often serve as education hubs while offering outreach solutions for recycling food waste.

- Native plant groups often have planting projects in need of funding and volunteers. Learn more about the plants native to your region, create immediate impact, and meet like-minded people.

- Do you have a botanic garden, outdoor club, nature center, ecology center, arboretum, or parks conservancy near you? Organizations like these increase the success of living greenways that ultimately connect our gardens to open space.

- Community gardens or allotments are another source of inspiration. Here you may find a plot to tend, workshops, and an opportunity to green your community while growing some of your own flowers and food.

- Are there places for kids to garden in your community? Perhaps at a school garden, community center, botanic garden, or with an organization like the LA Children's Garden? If not, there's no time like the present to get one started. The benefits of learning the language of nature and growing from a young age are far-reaching and invaluable.

We can maintain the status quo or grow a brighter future by going beyond organic, thinking like an ecosystem, and coauthoring a new narrative. Uplifting words and tools for best practices, such as *regenerative gardening* or *carbon gardening*, are a lens for seeing and rediscovering our one and only Planet A.

A NEW NORMAL

Somewhere along the way between planting, composting, and recording bumblebee sightings, a shift happens. It's an internal shift that is in itself a new normal—a new lens for seeing and being in the world. While life changing on a personal level, this new normal is essential for solving big issues like climate change.

WORDS AND PHRASES TO CULTIVATE A NEW NORMAL

rewild

revive

restore

resilient

regenerate

nurture

nourish

Nature equity

nature-based

mind open

hope

habitat

grow more good

green

gratitude

generosity

empower

do more good

curiosity

cultivate

courage

contribute

connectivity

compassion

collaborate

cocreate

coauthor

beyond organic

better together

I get that the climate crisis problem is huge and species extinction an alarm bell unlike any other, but it's here. It's happening. On a mass scale, we need to look to solutions such as shifting to renewable energy, transforming conventional agriculture into regenerative agriculture, and setting aside large tracts of land for nature—and fast. But even these solutions require an internal shift and a willingness to adopt an alternate lens that is inherently a deeply personal process.

Which brings us back home.

I've learned there are two ways lasting personal growth is achieved and a new normal is established: direct confrontation or practice. Direct confrontation comes with often dramatic and sometimes terrible experiences, experiences like car accidents, the death of a loved one, or living through a wildfire, hurricane, or pandemic. It's an experience that shakes you to the core, so much so that things can't go back to normal. Life and your worldview are forever changed. In comparison, a practice is just that, practice. It entails intentional and regular acts like meditation, yoga, adopting a mantra, or daily journaling or haiku. But really, a practice is anything that helps quiet and focus the mind, bringing you back to center while providing clarity and therefore an opportunity for growth, original thought, and an overall sense of well-being.

The simple act of growing and living close to nature is a practice and an opportunity for personal growth with collective impact.

The saying "change begins at home" is a literal one. It starts one garden at a time. And once you begin quite literally growing the change you want to see, you've started a conversation that when shared with others begins to find its way into the global conversation.

Nature needs us to act now, and if we're all doing one small part, the collective benefits reverberate across the globe. Like the flapping of a butterfly's wings.

Change begins at home, one garden at a time.

HELPFUL RESOURCES

If you're looking to deepen your knowledge, volunteer, or find the resources needed to grow your own carbon-friendly, biodiversity-rich garden, here are a few suggestions.

ORGANIZATIONS

Many larger, international organizations such as The Nature Conservancy and the Xerces Society have local chapters offering workshops and citizen science opportunities. Even the Surfrider Foundation has an Ocean Friendly Gardens program—look for it if you live along the coast.

American Horticultural Society
Australian National Botanic Gardens
Australian Network for Plant
    Conservation Inc.
Conservation International
E.O. Wilson Biodiversity Foundation
Fibershed
France Nature Environnement
Global Soil Partnership
Green America
Earth Guardians

Environmental Working Group
KidsGardening
Kiss the Ground
Irish Wildlife Trust
Landscape South Australia
Little Green Space (UK)
Monarch Watch
National Audubon Society
National Wildlife Federation
One Percent for the Planet
Pesticide Action Network
Rodale Institute
Save Our Soils
Sierra Club
Soil Association (UK)
speakGreen
Surfrider Foundation, Ocean Friendly
    Gardens program
The Nature Conservancy
The Royal Horticultural Society (UK)
The Wildlife Trusts (UK)
United Nations (UN)
    Intergovernmental Panel on Climate
    Change (IPCC)
UN Climate Action, UN Climate
    Action Summit, UN Environment
    Programme
UN Food and Agriculture Organization
Wildlife Conservation Society

World Wildlife Fund

Xerces Society

BOOKS

Berry, Wendell. *What Are People For?: Essays.* Berkeley, CA: Counterpoint, 2010.

Brown, Gabe. *Dirt to Soil: One Family's Journey into Regenerative Agriculture.* White River Junction, VT: Chelsea Green, 2018.

Carson, Rachel. *Silent Spring.* Boston, MA: Houghton Mifflin, 1962.

Dowding, Charles. *Charles Dowding's No Dig Gardening Course 1: From Weeds to Vegetables Easily and Quickly.* Somerset, UK: No Dig Garden, 2020.

Global Peace Initiative of Women, ed. *Sacred Seed.* Point Reyes, CA: Golden Sufi Center Publishing, 2014.

Goulson, Dave. *The Garden Jungle: or Gardening to Save the Planet.* London, UK: Vintage, 2020.

———. *Gardening for Bumblebees: A Practical Guide to Creating a Paradise for Pollinators.* Rochester, UK: Vintage Digital, 2021.

Howard, Brigit Strawbridge. *Dancing with Bees: A Journey Back to Nature.* White River Junction, VT: Chelsea Green, 2019.

Jacke, Dave, and Eric Toensmeier. *Edible Forest Gardens* (2-volume set). White River Junction, VT: Chelsea Green, 2005.

Kimmerer, Robin Wall. *Braiding Sweetgrass: Indigenous Wisdom, Scientific Knowledge and the Teachings of Plants.* Minneapolis, MN: Milkweed Editions, 2015.

Louie, Rebecca. *Compost City: Practical Composting Know-How for Small-Space Living.* Boulder, CO: Roost Books, 2015.

Lowenfels, Jeff. *Teaming with Fungi: The Organic Gardener's Guide to Mycorrhizae.* Portland, OR: Timber Press, 2017.

———, and Wayne Lewis. *Teaming with Microbes: The Organic Gardener's Guide to the Soil Food Web.* Revised edition. Portland, OR: Timber Press, 2010.

Miller, Daphne, MD. *Farmacology: Total Health from the Ground Up.* New York: William Morrow Paperbacks, 2016.

Montgomery, David R., and Anne Biklé. *The Hidden Half of Nature: The Microbial Roots of Life and Health.* New York: Norton, 2016.

Pollan, Michael. *Second Nature: A Gardener's Education.* New York: Grove Press, 2003.

Powers, Richard. *The Overstory: A Novel.* New York: Norton, 2019.

Rainer, Thomas, and Claudia West. *Planting in a Post-Wild World: Designing Plant Communities for Resilient Landscapes.* Portland, OR: Timber Press, 2015.

Schatzker, Mark. *The Dorito Effect: The Surprising New Truth About Food and Flavor.* New York: Simon & Schuster, 2016.

Tallamy, Douglas W. *Nature's Best Hope: A New Approach to Conservation That Starts in Your Yard.* Portland, OR: Timber Press, 2020.

Toensmeier, Eric. *Perennial Vegetables: From Artichoke to Zuiki Taro, a Gardener's Guide to Over 100 Delicious, Easy-to-Grow Edibles.* White River Junction, VT: Chelsea Green, 2007.

——, and Jonathan Bates. *Paradise Lot: Two Plant Geeks, One-Tenth of an Acre, and the Making of an Edible Garden Oasis in the City.* White River Junction, VT: Chelsea Green, 2013.

——. *The Carbon Farming Solution: A Global Toolkit of Perennial Crops and Regenerative Agriculture Practices for Climate Change Mitigation and Food Security.* White River Junction, VT: Chelsea Green, 2016.

Weaner, Larry, and Thomas Christopher. *Garden Revolution: How Our Landscapes Can Be a Source of Environmental Change.* Portland, OR: Timber Press, 2016.

Wilson, Edward O. *Half-Earth: Our Planet's Fight for Life.* New York: Liveright, 2017.

Wohlleben, Peter. *The Secret Wisdom of Nature: Trees, Animals, and the Extraordinary Balance of All Living Things—Stories from Science and Observation.* Vancouver, BC, Canada: Greystone Books, 2019.

MANY THANKS

I am one of the lucky ones. The community of people who fill my life and support my work is truly remarkable. Like with anything in life, this book would not have been possible without their presence and willingness to help. For this, I'm forever grateful.

To my editors, Stacee Lawrence and Lorraine Anderson, thank you for believing in me and for your thoughtful guidance. To the team at Timber Press, I'm honored to be one of your many authors as you work to provide a framework for all of us to grow a better world today and tomorrow.

To my family, Josh, Sinéad, and Madison, thank you for *everything*. Thanks to my mom, Maryann Hall, for sharing your love of growing. Thanks to my brother and his wife, Ron and Julie Perry, and extended family, Leon Hall, Grace and Mark Murphy, Kevin and Anne Murphy, and Christin and Ken Gould, for your generous support.

A huge thank you to the creatives and trailblazers in my life: Michael Jager, chief creative officer at Solidarity of Unbridled Labour; Will Raap, founder of Gardener's Supply and KidsGardening; Nicole Landers, cofounder of the Los Angeles Children's Garden; Robert Hewitt of Girasole Sonoma; Debbie Berne, Debbie Berne Design; and Dr. Claudia Gross of speakGreen. Thanks too to Charles Dowding for cheering me on and leading the way in no-dig gardening, and to Yvon Chouinard for encouraging me to read *The Dorito Effect* (a book integral to the shaping of this book) and leading the charge for regenerating our landscapes and lives.

Jeff and Doriana Hammond of West Cliff Creative, this book wouldn't be the same without your photographic support and collaboration. Thank you!

Sydney Loney, you are a star. Thank you for your editorial help and for giving me the courage to make this book. Sara Rasmussen, Jane Sievert, Elissa Fisher-Harris, Lorene Edwards Forkner, Carey Davidson, Marsi Foster, Meg Cowden, Kier Holmes, Jennifer Jewell, Kathryn Aalto, Andrew Sabatini, Steve Cameron, Marni Wandner, Sarah Alba, Kate Rutherford, Nicky English, Todd English, Amy Trapp, Andy Trapp, and Ellen Ecker Ogden, thank you for your encouragement and reminding me that we're better together.

To the women who took time out of their busy schedules to share research from their fields of soil science (Dr. Nicole Tautges and Dr. Jessica Chiartas), pollinator conservation (Dr. Shannon Westlake), and conservation psychology (Dr. Kayla Cranston), thank you. You have been integral to my research.

My cousin, Marcy Boom, along with Johanna Silver, and Deborah Miuccio of Gardener's Supply—you are amazing. Thanks so much for helping organize the many gardens I photographed.

And last but not least, to all of you who welcomed me into your gardens and farms to photograph—Eric Toensmeier, Todd Lynch, David Grist, Robert Hewitt, Pam Karlson, Joanna Letz of Bluma Flower Farm, Anita Rackerby, Michael Martinez of LA Compost, Nicole Landers, Danielle Marquez, Mud Baron, Leslie Bennett of Pine House Edible Gardens, Kelsey Adams of West Lane Flowers, Gardener's Supply, Cat Malone, Lauren Klein, Ruth Mainland, Lisa Barringer, Nicky and Todd English, and the Sonoma Garden Park and Ecology Center—thank you!

PHOTOGRAPHY CREDITS

West Cliff Creative, pages 2, 10, 13, 14, 15, 16, 19, 20 bottom, 21, 23, 31, 32, 33, 35, 41 top left, 48, 55, 62, 78 left, 99, 102, 118, 136 bottom, 137 top, 148, 156 right, 157 top left and right, 162 bottom left and right, 163, 171, 172 top right, middle, and bottom, 180, 190 right, 196 top, 213, 215, 222, 228, 233

Jonathan Murphy, page 162 top

Sinéad Murphy, page 190 left, 220 bottom

All other photos by the author.

INDEX

Emily Murphy is the author of the Amazon best seller *Grow What You Love* and a leading proponent of regenerative organic growing and garden-based climate activism. She's a practiced plantsperson, designer, educator, and photographer. As the grandchild of immigrants whose livelihoods were tied closely to the land, Emily had the opportunity to learn the wonder of natural systems and growing from an early age. She is the creator of the celebrated blog *Pass the Pistil* and has dedicated herself to nature-based garden education and nature advocacy. She has appeared on NBC's *Today* and the *Marilyn Denis Show,* and her writings can be found in *Better Homes and Gardens, the Saturday Evening Post, Mother Earth News,* and *Pacific Horticulture.* Emily's background in ethnobotany, ecology, soil science, and education gives her a unique ability to translate concepts of regenerative organics, carbon gardening, and biodiversity for the home gardener and community-driven initiatives. She lives with her family in coastal Northern California.